SHAI

D0106110

Transforming Scripture

TRANSFORMATIONS
THE EPISCOPAL CHURCH IN THE 21ST CENTURY

Transforming Scripture

FRANK WADE

CHURCH PUBLISHING
an imprint of Church Publishing Incorporated, New York

© 2008 by Frank Wade
All rights reserved.

No part of this book may be reproduced, stored in a retrieval system,
or transmitted in any form or by any means, electronic, mechanical,
including photocopying, recording, or otherwise, without the written
permission of the publisher.

Unless otherwise indicated, all passages from the scriptures are from
the *New Revised Standard Version* of the Bible. © 1989 by the
Division of Christian Education of the National Council of Churches
of Christ in the U.S.A. Used by permission. All rights reserved.

Library of Congress Cataloging-in-Publication Data
Wade, Frank.
Transforming Scripture / by Frank Wade.
    p.   cm. — (Transformations: the Episcopal Church in the 21st
century)
Includes bibliographical references.
ISBN 978-0-89869-594-6 (pbk.)
1. Bible—Criticism, interpretation, etc. 2. Episcopal Church—
Doctrines. I. Title.
BS511.3.W33 2008
                                    220.088'28373—dc22

Cover design by Stefan Killen Design.
Study guide and interior design by Vicki K. Black.

Printed in the United States of America.

Church Publishing, Incorporated
445 Fifth Avenue
New York, New York 10016
www.churchpublishing.com

        5   4   3   2   1

Contents

a note from the publisher

This series emerged as a partnership between the Office of Mission of the Episcopal Church and Church Publishing, as a contribution to the mission of the church in a new century. We would like to thank James Lemler, series editor, for bringing the initial idea to us and for facilitating the series. We also want to express our gratitude to the Office of Mission for two partnership grants: the first brought all the series authors together for two creative days of brainstorming and fellowship; and the second is helping to further publicize the books of the series to the clergy and lay people of the Episcopal Church.

Series Preface

"Be ye transformed" (KJV). "Be transformed by the renewing of your minds" (NRSV). "Fix your attention on God. You'll be changed from the inside out" (*The Message*). Thus St. Paul exhorted the earliest Christian community in his writing to the Romans two millennia ago. This exhortation was important for the early church and it is urgent for the Episcopal Church to heed as it enters the twenty-first century. Be transformed. Be changed from the inside out.

Perhaps no term fits the work and circumstances of the church in the twenty-first century better than "transformation." We are increasingly aware of the need for change as we become ever more mission-focused in the life of the church, both internationally and domestically. But society as a whole is rapidly moving in new directions, and mission cannot be embraced in an unexamined way, relying on old cultural and ecclesiastical stereotypes and assumptions.

This new series, *Transformations: The Episcopal Church in the 21st Century,* addresses these issues in realistic and hopeful ways. Each book focuses on one area within the Episcopal Church that is urgently in need of transformation in order for the church to be effective in the twenty-first century: vocation, evangelism, preaching, congregational life, getting to know the Bible, leadership, Christian formation, worship, and stewardship. Each volume explains why a changed vision is essential, gives robust theological and biblical foundations, offers guidelines to best practices and positive trends, describes the necessary tools for change, and imagines how transformation will look.

Most Episcopalians will readily admit to not knowing the Bible and are reluctant to engage the scriptures in a disciplined and regular way. We often hear the Bible only on Sundays, and even then it is heard in the context of the liturgy—through the words of the Book of Common Prayer and Hymnal—and interpreted through sermons. In this volume Frank Wade explores what lies behind our reluctance to let the Bible's power transform us in the essentially spiritual process of inquiring after God. How can the Bible bring about congregational and personal transformation? How do we read the Bible as a "revealed text," the Word of God, in such widely differing contexts and remain faithful to Anglicanism's hermeneutic of scripture?

Like Christians in the early church, today we live in a secular culture that can be apathetic and even hostile to Christianity. Living in a setting where people are not familiar with the message or narrative of Christian believing requires new responses and new kinds of mission for the Body of Christ. We believe this is a hopeful time for spiritual seekers and inquirers in the church. The gospel itself is fresh for this century. God's love is vibrant and real; God's mission can transform people's hopes and lives. Will we participate in the transformation? Will we be bearers and agents of transformation for others? Will we ourselves be transformed? This is the call and these are the urgent questions for the Episcopal Church in the twenty-first century.

But first, seek to be transformed. Fix your attention on God. You'll be changed from the inside out.

JAMES B. LEMLER, *series editor*

Acknowledgments

Being in community is one of the tangible joys of our faith. In the course of writing this book, I have been blessed, guided, informed, challenged, and supported by a wonderful congregation of colleagues, friends, and family.

Philip Cato and Richard Busch helped me to frame the broad outlines of the book.

Carlton Hayden, Charles Kiblinger, William Barnwell, Joseph Clark, Diana Smith, Ginny Doctor, Margot Critchfield, James Simon, Ian Douglas, and Harriette Sturges helped me to understand the various Bible study programs.

Janine Tinsley-Roe, Winfred Vergara, and Anthony Guillén of the national church staff in New York were especially helpful in explaining some of the opportunities available in new understandings of diversity, as was my colleague at General Seminary, Juan Oliver.

The staff at Virginia Theological Seminary, especially Amy Dyer and Dorothy Linthicum in the Center for the Ministry of Teaching, and librarian Mitzi Budde, were most generous.

The wonderful storytellers who contributed to the final chapter are each named in context but deserve a separate note of thanks for their insights and candor.

Cynthia Shattuck has been a wise and faithful editor.

My wife Mary is to be thanked for her extravagant gifts of patience while I was writing and for being the joy of my life when I was not.

Finally, this book is dedicated to the people of the church of the twenty-first century, specifically Lila McCleer Greiner, Henry Wade Greiner, Jackson Carlisle Wade, and Kathryn Valerie Wade. May they find and be found by God at the great meeting ground.

chapter one

The Bible as Meeting Ground

In 1699 the Bishop of London dispatched the Reverend Thomas Bray to the wilds of Maryland to see how the Anglican Church was doing. His report, dated 1701, was pessimistic: "They are in very much want of instruction in the Christian religion, and in some of them utterly destitute of the same." To Bray's credit he addressed the problem by establishing the Society for the Propagation of the Gospel, which provided missionary support throughout the British Empire and continues to serve to this day, but success in biblical literacy continues to elude Episcopalians just as it does the rest of the population of the United States. Stephen Prothero, historian of religion and popular culture at Boston University, tells us in *Religious Literacy* that while Americans hold the most widespread belief in the supernatural of any developed country, we are the most religiously ignorant in the Western world. A recent Gallup poll contains the stark revelation that we remain "a nation of biblical illiterates," with half of our adult population unable to name even one of the four gospels. If this is the result of three centuries of teaching, it might be time for a different approach.

There is good news and bad news about the way Episcopalians approach Holy Scripture. The good news is that we who worship weekly and on the feast days of the church probably hear *more* scripture read and expounded upon—in prayers, sermons, and hymns—than many other mainline Protestants. The bad news is that our once-a-week (at best) liturgical engagement with scripture is all most Episcopalians get. This is something most of us know to be true. Indeed, our lack of disciplined scriptural engagement is one of the inside jokes most Episcopalians chuckle about in moments of self-deprecating honesty.

Most Episcopalians will readily admit to not knowing the scriptures. Some will even describe a personal reluctance to engage the Bible in disciplined study for reasons ranging from simple apathy to a complex and fearful aversion. Not surprisingly, the 1999 Zaccheus Report by the Episcopal Church Foundation affirmed that the scriptures are clearly *less* central to the faith life of the majority of Episcopalians than the Prayer Book, hymnal, and Holy Eucharist.

In this book I will consider some of the reasons why to this day Episcopalians are still "in very much want of instruction" in the Bible, as well as in some of the foundations upon which a new and transformative approach could be based. Beginning with past and current approaches to scripture in our church, I will suggest a new emphasis that may allow the Bible to bear more fruit in us now than it has in the past. I say "emphasis" rather than "technique" because I think this is more a matter of soul and heart than of method, even though the right tools are important. (We will look at some of these later on.) So recognizing that we are a people who like to "cut to the chase," I am going to summarize in the briefest possible terms just what that emphasis will be. That way you can have some idea of where we are going, and we can travel together harmoniously without worrying too much about the destination.

Christianity is not basically a philosophy or a body of knowledge but a way of living in which we meet and experience the living God. Consequently its primary resource, the Bible, misses its potential when it is considered apart from living our lives in relationship with God. The Bible is a meeting ground where our spiritual ancestors have gone for the past several thousand years to encounter the Lord and see their lives deepened and directed in accordance with God's priorities. The "meeting" which takes place in these holy texts has consistently proven to contain infinite human value, even as our perceptions and understandings of the "meeting ground" have changed. The study of scripture provides us with a guidebook to this place of meeting, telling us of origins, interpretations, and nuances that help us to hear the Word the Lord is speaking. In the same way that a museum audio-tour helps us to observe a painting all the more closely, or a theater program helps us to understand a play, Bible study opens us to the fullest experience of God in scripture. It is possible to be so poorly prepared and biblically illiterate that we can hear almost nothing from God, while the clamor of our culture comes through loud and clear. And it is possible for the wrong kind of study to make the encounter so full of bits of information that we hear nothing but reverberations and echoes—think of a restaurant with so much rattle and clatter that conversation is reduced to lip reading.

The whole point of the religious enterprise is to be in a right relationship with God. William James wrote over a century ago in *The Varieties of Religious Experience* that religious belief, Christianity included, holds that "there is something wrong with us as we naturally stand" and that "we are saved from that wrongness by making proper connection with the higher powers." Our approach to the Bible must reach for that "proper connection" or there is no reason to approach it all.

While our "want of instruction" is still daunting, this book will show that we are perfectly poised to alter our course and make the desired connection. I will take a candid look at the issues that seem to confuse our church, and then consider the theological foundations that have been provided for us by our forebears—as well as what our contemporaries have built upon them with renewed Bible study methods and systems. I want to show how our best traditions can be extended into the twenty-first century, allowing us to be sufficiently informed and enriched by scripture to let the soul of Thomas Bray rest more easily.

Now that you have some idea of where we are going, let's consider what is involved in getting there.

---

challenges from the culture

I grew up in West Virginia just after World War II. An annual feature of public school life was a Christmas pageant: shepherds in potato sacks, citizens in bathrobes, kings swathed in bolts of cloth, angels in white, and serious competition over the roles of Gabriel and Mary. During the year, those who chose to were allowed to leave school early and walk across town to the Methodist Church for classes titled "Religious Education." This was, of course, more an education by the dominant culture than true public education. My hometown was overwhelmingly Christian and, at that time, had little concern for the fine points of the separation of church and state.

Without considering whether these programs were good or bad, we need to acknowledge that they are things of the past. While there are some attempts in the academy to honor the literary heritage of the Bible with courses like "The Bible as Literature," our schools, for reasons well beyond the scope of this book, have pretty well gone out of the Bible story business. Of course the school was not always diligent in its faithfulness to the fullness of the biblical narrative. What was offered was clumsy, selective, and shallow, but by acting out the Christmas story and allotting time in the curriculum for what was essentially Bible school, the school system and the community it served bore witness to the value of knowing the Bible. Our diverse culture is wisely silent on the faith story of any one group. Nevertheless, in that silence the Christian community must increase its efforts and effectiveness in making the Bible an option for those who would know the Lord. The Episcopal Church, which has historically been so identified with the surrounding culture and has never developed a zeal for personal witness, is faced with particular challenges in sharing the importance of the Bible with its own members and beyond.

We live in times that are far from reflective and quiet, and there are many more voices laying claim to our attention than in days gone by. We live in what is often called "The Information Age," which affords us many benefits as well as widening and deepening our sense of confusion. The information we receive from television and the internet, news and advertising media, church and state, principalities and powers is constant and virtually unfiltered. The Information Age has no method, and apparently little interest, in distinguishing between good information and bad, rumor and fact, urban legend and formative myth. We need something to help us sort the miraculous from the ridiculous, revelations from aberrations, mystery from mayhem, the ordinary from the extraordinary. The Episcopal Church, by virtue of education, income, and interest, tends to be well in touch with this undisciplined media flow and so is particularly in need of the kind of grounding the Bible has traditionally provided.

Episcopalians do need some way to be reminded of who we are and of knowing what we are supposed to do. In fact we need our church to be the "family" we often describe it to be. Families, clans, and tribes have historically provided their members with two essential formative gifts. One is identity, and the second is training in the kinds of behavior that characterize that identity. It is through our family that we are told who we are—what our roots are, whether we be European or Asian, first-generation or tenth-generation, white-collar or blue-collar. And we are taught what it means to express that identity in our daily lives. We learn about forks or chopsticks, manners and skills, lore and heritage. In a similar way, the church family needs to impart more clearly the identity that is rooted in our baptism, the behaviors required by its covenant and the rich lore that has sustained our "family" for centuries. For many generations the Bible provided that identity and guide but it is increasingly difficult to hear its message amid the cacophony of voices that fill our screens, radios, newspapers, and iPods. The Bible still speaks and the church still interprets its message, but only those who really *work* at listening can hear what is being said.

Our ancestors generally had the opposite problem: too little data. And for many centuries the information they had was drawn from the Bible, for the Word of the Lord was almost the only word they had. That "word" can certainly be found in the contemporary mix of blogs, bluster, blasphemy, and solid reporting, but it is very difficult for the average person to recognize. Jesus once said that his sheep would know his voice. That is a comforting thought, but I doubt that we can assume that we ourselves will recognize his voice as a natural byproduct of baptism. If we are going to recognize the Lord's voice, it will be the way sheep and other creatures do—by listening. We must listen to it, become familiar with it, and then and only then we will be able to recognize it.

> The one who enters by the gate is the shepherd of the sheep. The gatekeeper opens the gate for him, and the sheep hear his voice. He calls his own sheep by name and leads them out. When he has brought out all his own, he goes ahead of them, and the sheep follow him because they know his voice. *(John 10:2–4)*

That calls for a renewed investment in Bible reading on the part of Episcopalians. Where else can we learn the sound of God's "voice" apart from scripture? How would we know our identity as children of God apart from the struggles and triumphs of those who have gone before us? How will we know what to do in a noisy, shifting, morphing world unless we know the priorities, interests, and instincts of God? Where will we learn those things apart from what generations have come to call the Word of the Lord? It is true that we hear lessons read every Sunday and usually hear them interpreted from the pulpit, but few of us have the kind of immersion in scripture that will bring us to the meeting ground and allow us to hear the Lord's voice. We know we are Christians, but that is not enough. Without God's voice we are like sheep without a shepherd, seeds thrown on hard ground, or fools before dumb idols. The unhappy lot of all of these is well described in scripture, as are the virtues of a mustard seed, the widow's mite, and those who soar on eagle's wings. Hearing God's Word in a world of too much information is not easy—but it is essential.

Besides the competing racket all around us, Episcopalians (like everyone else) are questioning the frameworks and measuring rods that provided a source of clarity for previous generations. Those who keep track of the world's trends tell us that we are living in a "post-modern" age. The significant thing about that description is that it says nothing about what is going on—except that it is not like it was before. We have emerged from a way of understanding that was called "modern" and find ourselves in a nameless wilderness that is so new and vague that it is called literally "that-which-comes-after-modern." There are few if any norms or basic assumptions upon which we universally rely. Individuals have their certainties, to be sure. You have some and so do I. But as a whole, as a culture, we do not. Our world is like a shattered mirror, a Humpty Dumpty that is not going to come back together the way that it was before. Globalization and multiculturalism are only two forces among the many new influences on society at large.

The Episcopal Church's call to greater and wider diversity is requiring not only a second look, but also a reexamination and reordering of longstanding norms and practices. The fact that the current disputes in the Episcopal Church are focused on core issues such as the interpretation of scripture, the authority of bishops, and the meaning of morality indicates new examinations of old assumptions, a very postmodern sort of thing. Suffice it to say that "the times, they are a-changing," and nobody is quite sure what they are changing into. The old norms, standards, and reliable resources seem inadequate to the tasks of the age and are being set aside without an obvious new set of trusted guides at hand. One of the casualties of this newness is the Bible, which previously had to be reckoned with by anyone who wanted to be taken seriously about business, politics, family life, or foreign relations. Now it is often ignored even by those who write about ethics and morality. Faithful people who take the Bible seriously must do so in a world that no longer does.

The questioning of most norms and basic assumptions is important for many reasons that are beyond the scope of this book, but there is one basic assumption that we should pause and take note of. Our God is the Creator who has never stopped building a "new thing" on ancient foundations. This was one of the remarkable revelations received by our ancestors. The ancient world could see the cyclical patterns of nature and assumed that history worked the same way. The human story, they reasoned, simply repeated itself over and over the way the moon, the Nile, and the seasons did. The first words of the Bible, however, challenge that assumption and set us off in what was then an entirely new direction: "In the beginning" is a stunning blow to the idea that life goes in circles because circles do not have beginnings. Our spiritual ancestors declared with God's own authority that life's story has a beginning and thus a middle and an end. We now accept such a notion as commonplace, but it certainly was not in its day. Among other things it introduced us to the concept of the future, of newness, of God's plan for creation, and of God's creatures as continuously "unfolding." That revelation allows us to be called followers of Jesus—because Jesus is going somewhere and we can never quite be certain of the direction. Our faith is a rich combination of old and new, with the clear admonition to avoid putting new wine in old wineskins. Christianity is alive and bubbling with the creative energy of God.

To join in that creative enterprise, we need to have solid foundations, such as a thorough knowledge of scripture, because the difference between creativity and chaos is the presence of a standard, a norm. Creativity is a departure from the baseline of routine and common assumptions. Where these are missing we have not creativity but chaos—where even the best minds can only wander from one novelty to another like crows picking up shiny objects with no value other than their glitter. Consider that the Sunday liturgy has a basic pattern that still allows us to do different things that inform, enrich, and delight (as well as occasionally irritate) us. If the liturgy were different every Sunday, we would end up deeply unsatisfied.

On a much larger scale, the whole church may lose its ability to be truly creative, and therefore informative, enriching, and delightful, if it lacks sufficient norms of identity, authority, or belief to keep it out of chaos. This is not God's intent for us. You will recall that in the creation story the Spirit of God broods over chaos (a "multi-verse") and brings it into order (a "uni-verse"). That is the act of choosing order over disorder, creativity over commotion. God's plan is not for creatures to be in lockstep but that we should have enough of a common thread, a baseline for the creation to share in the joy of creativity. Every sunrise is not alike, but all sunrises have enough in common for us to know what they are. Every person is unique, but we are all called to common tasks of giving, receiving, loving, and living. Our age, and with it our church, is in some danger of losing its common thread, and with it our capacity for true creativity.

This is important because God has generously invited us to join in the unfolding of creation. We are stewards of the earth and its resources; the garden is ours to till. We are given enormous and sometimes frightening freedom to build up or destroy people, relationships, and communities—to say nothing of art, insight, and education. We can build temples to the holy that help us to know our real place in life or towers of Babel that merely serve our vanity and delusion. We can make war or love or peace or mayhem. Whether we join in the creative enterprise or simply collect shiny objects depends on the presence of life-tested norms, assumptions, and baselines.

What we actually do, wittingly or unwittingly, depends on whom we follow, for life only goes in one direction, and that is forward into a future unknown to us. Those who discount traditional norms and fail to mark the trail of those who can lead us into the future are opting for chaos. Those who grab hold of the ancient expressions of truth as if they were rocks in a turbulent stream are choosing to opt out of the future and stay in a world already made and safely explored. The twenty-first century will not reward either approach. The ancient truths must be taken more seriously, not less so. We must learn to hear the heart of their wisdom, not just their outer form or earliest implications. We must remember that the wisdom of the past is precious to us because of what it says about the present and the future. The dividing line between today and tomorrow remains the only point where we can actively accept God's invitation to be followers and co-creators. Our ability to know the Lord's familiar voice in unfamiliar places is the key to stepping into the future and helping to shape it.

challenges within the Episcopal Church

The Episcopal Church certainly shares in the broader cultural disconnect with scripture but we also have some issues of our own that serve to perpetuate our ignorance of the Bible and make us oblivious to its power. What makes the situation more complicated is that these same issues are among our greatest strengths. They are things we tend to like about ourselves and could not let go of and still think of ourselves as Episcopalians. I am thinking especially of our sense of social responsibility, our high regard for education, and our Sunday lectionary.

A high regard for social justice is in the DNA of the Episcopal Church. It is also rooted in our history as the state church of England and its empire; in that role the

Anglican Church cared for the poor, its clergy served as community health officers, and its lay ministries were the ultimate recourse for widows and orphans. When the state of Virginia disestablished the Anglican Church after the Revolutionary War, its leaders found that they had to create the civil office of Overseer of the Poor to fulfill what had been the church's role. The briefest glance at the life of our church in any era will amply show our concern for the poor, the hungry, the recovering, and the homeless— few of whom are worshipping members. How could such a jewel in our crown be a problem? It is the Bible that tells us to care for the sojourner and to find Jesus in the least among us, so how could such practices separate us from the Bible's power?

Like good stewards of the manifold grace of God, serve one another with whatever gift each of you has received. *(1 Peter 4:10)*

The problem is that we Episcopalians take this biblical mandate so much for granted that we don't take the time to study or seriously critique it. Our outreach ministries are an honest reaction to what we see in the world around us, but they arise as much from ordinary philanthropy as from hard listening to God's Word. We act without the benefit of serious reflection on how addressing poverty and injustice might fit into the saving narratives of scripture, or be rooted in God's continuing revelation. Assuming that the demand to respond to social evils is absolute, we see no need to wait for a response to emerge from our reading of scripture.

No one can argue against the goal of social responsibility and I am certainly not trying to do so here. But because we do not study the scriptures, we have a knee-jerk response to social concerns. The problem is compounded by the fact that we, as a church, no longer require our outreach programs to be based on any serious study of scripture. Thousands of Episcopalians are involved in outreach, but how many are able to articulate the biblical reasons for doing so? Returning to those biblical roots might redirect some of our efforts. The prophet Amos talks about the unequal distribution of wealth, the breakdown of compassion for the poor, and unethical business practices. Jesus talks about the spiritually deadening effect of wealth. The Bible still has much to say to us, but we have stopped listening because we are so busy running thrift shops and making sandwiches. We see a need in the world and we go after it, which is a good thing, but we usually content ourselves with addressing the symptoms of poverty rather than its causes, hacking at the branches of evil rather than striking the root. That may in fact be all that God expects of us, but if it were more—or otherwise—how would we know?

One reason for this lack of rootedness in the Bible may be that the Baptismal Covenant has become the major authority and foundation for putting our faith into practice. Church leaders who call us to social responsibility do not ground their exhortations in the wider biblical story, but consistently turn to the Baptismal Covenant, particularly the fifth question: "Will you strive for justice and peace among all people, and respect the dignity of every human person?" (BCP 305). According to the Standing Commission on Ministry Development, all ministries in the Episcopal Church are now seen as "grounded in the baptismal covenant" and revisions to ministry canons "should support this foundation."[1] So, for example, in 2006 the Executive Council took a position on immigration laws and that same year the General Convention advocated for wider registration drives. In 2007 a major conference on the United Nations Millennium Development Goals was convened; later that year, a significant session of the National Episcopal AIDS Coalition was held. What these initiatives have in common is their reliance on the Baptismal Covenant as the source of their mandate for action. These are all worthwhile initiatives that deserve our full support and enthusiasm; my point is that the Baptismal Covenant is becoming, or perhaps has become, the "Summary of the Gospel" for Episcopalians, just as Mark 12:29–31 is the Summary of the Law.

Liturgical scholar Marian Hatchett reminds us in his *Commentary on the American Prayer Book* that rites of initiation always provide models for other events in a culture because initiation is the central liturgy for the community.[2] Our enthusiasm for the Baptismal Covenant is understandable in light of Hatchett's teaching. It is a beautiful, comprehensive, and compelling summary, but it is still a summary, and I wonder if it has come to stand between us and the full, vital texts of scripture. Perhaps one reason we do not trouble ourselves to search out scripture's theological rationale for service (whether it is for immigration reform or the search for an AIDS vaccine) is that we have the covenant so readily at hand. It has become our CliffsNotes for the Bible—all we really need to know in eight simple questions, with five of them having the same answer. The covenant is fruitful, but it is the branch, not the vine, and to ensure its continued fruitfulness we must keep it connected to its source of meaning.

It is no secret that education is greatly prized among Episcopalians; it may even be called one of our defining values. Our clergy are expected to satisfy rigorous academic demands prior to ordination, and on the whole our congregations are well-educated. The best traditions of Anglicanism are set in solid reasoning. Theologically sound biblical criticism has been one of our touchstones since the Reformation; we held on to it during the anti-intellectual emotionalism of the Great Awakenings of the nineteenth century and the fundamentalist controversies of the twentieth. We are not likely to let this priority go in the twenty-first century, nor should we.

But, as Saint Paul told the Corinthians, "The kingdom of God depends not on talk but on power" (1 Corinthians 4:20). His point is one we are in some danger of missing as we concentrate on intellectual probing and scholarly reflection. If your experience is anything like mine, most of the classes and sermons Episcopalians hear on the Bible focus on its content without exposing its power to change our lives. As I noted above, Christianity is not basically a philosophy or a body of knowledge, but a way of living in which we meet and experience the living God. For many of us, reading the Bible is an exercise of the mind. In the thirteenth century Thomas Aquinas wrote that three things were necessary for salvation: we must know what we ought to believe, know what we ought to desire, and know what we ought to do. The word *know* is repeated three times; at the heart of Aquinas's theology is the belief that exercising reason will lead us into truth.

Similarly, in our day we acquire knowledge about the Bible, study this or that passage, parse the Greek or Hebrew words behind the English translation, and learn the difference between the Saul who became king and the Saul who became Paul. Not only is there nothing wrong with such an approach, one must be wary of any approach to scripture that takes such study lightly. Richard Hooker, one of the sixteenth-century founders of our own tradition, made the use of reason one of the central pillars of Anglicanism. But the exercise of intellect is finally just that: an approach. It is what brings us to the meeting ground, but not the experience of meeting the living God.

Our own studies, ponderings, discussions, and meditations must be held in a similar balance. To move from the heavy lifting of Aquinas's scholasticism to something a little closer to home, the Bible is like a book about swimming. Such a book could tell us much about the physics of water displacement, the manner in which various aquatic creatures move about, the disciplines of Olympic athletes, and the joys of pool and pond. But the study of swimming can take us just so far. At some point the book must be put down and the water entered. Our own faith seeks such a moment.

As a Prayer Book collect has been reminding us since 1549, we seek to "hear..., read, mark, learn, and inwardly digest" the scriptures (BCP 184/236). We often cover the first four and stop short of the fifth because scholarship can only take us so far. Our unwillingness or inability to follow through on Thomas Cranmer's prayer will leave us frustrated until we recognize that learning prepares us to meet the Lord and is no substitute for it.

Blessed Lord, who caused all holy Scriptures to be written for our learning: Grant us so to hear them, read, mark, learn, and inwardly digest them, that we may embrace and ever hold fast the blessed hope of everlasting life, which you have given us in our Savior Jesus Christ. *—The Book of Common Prayer*

Lectionary worship is a fixed star in our cosmos, and Episcopalians take real pride in the fact that regular worshippers in our churches hear as much scripture as they do every Sunday and feast day. When we add the prayers, hymns, sermons, and canticles with all their biblical allusions, our exposure is even more significant. If the Bible were radioactive we would all glow in the dark. But the Bible is not and we remain largely in the dark about the Bible and its contents. How can this be?

If we consider the important distinction between breadth and depth we may begin to get the picture. On a typical Sunday we hear three lessons, perhaps a psalm, maybe a canticle or two. Several clichés come to mind: trying to drink from a fire hose...too much of a good thing... *mas despachio, por favor*...Enough, already! Our regular Sunday outpouring of scripture is ambitious in its scope, largely unfiltered in its presentation, and often not clearly heard by the congregation. Is it any wonder that such a routine fails to inform, much less enrich and empower? The popular practice of printing scripture texts in the bulletin is helpful but not enough to add comparable depth to our almost incomprehensible breadth. Taking the time to find a special piece of God's truth in the Sunday readings, whether the preacher chooses to speak on it or not, is worth doing before or after the church service. It is also almost the only way to even begin to "inwardly digest" the Sunday readings.

No one will be able to convince us that social irresponsibility, lack of learning, and fewer readings will bring us to the foot of the cross. Their opposites, which we value so much, must never be taken away. But they can be added to. Patiently letting our call to serve the world in Christ's name rise from scripture; boldly letting the heart take over when the mind has reached its limit; and carefully choosing a single nugget from the Sunday stream are the tasks before us. Failure to do so is keeping us biblically illiterate.

challenges within the Bible

The Bible is clearly intended to provide a baseline for living creatively, for knowing and following the Lord into the future, and for letting us experience the living God. This is why it is common practice for those arguing for one side or another of a theological position always to call on scripture as the support—if not the absolute mandate—for their assumptions and beliefs. This is common because it is so easily done: the Bible is absolutely prodigal in its support for all kinds of causes across the ethical divide. All we need do is remember scripture's untroubled acceptance of slavery, which was used to justify that institution for centuries on the part of pro-slavery Anglicans. We need not wonder that the Devil was able to quote from holy writ as he tempted Jesus in the wilderness. The Bible calls us to both conformity and rebellion, quiet reflection and bold action, embrace of the new and adherence to the old, wise prudence and prodigal extravagance, fear and trust, hard justice and tender mercy. It is easy for almost any human impulse to find justification in the words of scripture. The Bible is in many ways like a person: if you torture it long enough you can get it to say almost anything. The Bible's record of apparent support for so many good and bad ideas should give us pause as we turn to it for guidance. Hearing God's voice in scripture when it is so obvious that others have heard a completely opposing voice is one of the first challenges we find within the Bible. I will consider ways to wrestle with these challenges later on, but for now honesty requires an acknowledgment that the danger is real.

In addition to its ambiguous and somewhat pliable nature, the Bible offers other challenges for any twenty-first-century reader. One obvious complication is the difference in the way ancient writers and modern readers view the physical universe in which the story takes place. Our spiritual ancestors understood the universe to be a simple place with the earth at its center, the star studded dome of heaven above it, and an abyss or pit, Sheol, below it. They could speak of God "above," of Christ "entering" this world and then "ascending into heaven," of people going "down" to Sheol. All of these images and actions depended on the simple three-story universe our ancestors imagined.

We, on the other hand, know earth to be a fragile little island in a "vast expanse of interstellar space," while heaven and hell are neither "up" nor "down." We have to think poetically and not literally in order to get the descriptions of our ancestors to work for us. This can be done because the Bible is, after all, not a science book but a revelation of the true nature of God and God's people. Almost all of its language is more metaphor than measure, more imagery than photography. God "enters" our world because God loves us. Christ "ascends" because he is of the same substance as God and belongs with God. People go "down" because what we do in this life really matters in the next. The stage directions behind those truths are not the most important thing, but they do require the modern mind to reach beyond the surface of some biblical texts in order to touch the meaning of them.

Inasmuch as the Bible provides us with a story of the people of God and what scholars call "salvation history," we must deal with an understanding of "history" that is very different from our own. You and I expect history to be an accurate record upon which we put our own interpretation or "stamp"; in other words, we reserve the right to make our own judgments about the importance or meaning of the events. This approach, which makes so much sense to us, has only been around since the Renaissance. During the long period in which the Bible was being written down, and for centuries before and afterward, history was understood to be the exact opposite. Ancient chroniclers, including the gospel writers, told us the theological meaning of events without worrying too much about what our modern minds would call "objectivity" or the details of the historical record.

The author of the gospel of John provides the clearest example of this approach when he asserts that his gospel is "written so that you may come to believe that Jesus is the Messiah" (John 20:31). In other words, the author *knows* that Jesus is the Messiah and he is telling the story so that the reader will come to the same conclusion. Luke begins his gospel in a similar vein, citing his own serious investigations and desire to set forth an "orderly account." But his intent, like John's, is that the reader "may know the truth" (Luke 1:1–4). A glimpse at the gospel of Luke reveals, however, that this truth is not based on a dispassionate review of the story from the perspective of Pharisees as well as the disciples, or from interviews with the Sadducees and with Mary, Jesus' mother. It is a proclamation of Luke's own belief that Jesus is the Messiah.

Furthermore, while the approach and conclusions of the gospels are consistent, the details often seem tangled to us. When we read in three of the gospels that Jesus cleansed the temple in the last week of his public ministry, but according to the fourth gospel it was done in the first week, we want to ask these evangelists to get their act together! But if we could call them all to account, they would have trouble understanding our problem, as all four are indicating that cleansing the temple was a highly symbolic act that characterized Jesus' public ministry. Their common point is its true significance, and whether that point is made by placing it first or last makes little difference. Once again we moderns have to stretch to know what the ancients are trying to say.

We must cease to treat the phraseology, the forms, definitions, and dogmas of Christianity as sacred relics, too sacred to be handled. We must take them out of their napkins ... and turn them into current coin. We must let them do business in the life that is living now.
— *William Porcher DuBose*

Of course, what is important to us now is not to know what Matthew and Luke and Isaiah and Paul are trying to tell us, but what *God* is saying to us through them. As enriching as it might be to come to know a leader like Nehemiah or a tough talker like James, it is an encounter with God that we seek. And when we go to the meeting ground of scripture seeking the "proper connection" with God, we come up against the natural limitations of theological language. We have no words for God. They all have to be borrowed from somewhere else—in other words, metaphors. We say that God is like one thing or another—lord or love, shepherd or wind—but none of our words point directly at God the way the word "tree" points to the one in the front yard. We need something more than words or words about words to help us find God in the meeting ground.

In the lovely and intricate writing of our fourth president, James Madison, "When the Almighty himself condescends to mankind in their own language, His meaning, luminous as it must be, is rendered doubtful by the cloudy medium through which it is communicated." Madison gives us two significant points. The first is that if God communicates with us at all, much of God's original intent must be left out because there are no words adequate to carry the meaning. In the same way, explaining something to a small child must be limited to a child's vocabulary. The second point is that if we have trouble unraveling a two-hundred-year-old sentence by James Madison, we must expect to struggle with two-*thousand*-year-old sentences by our spiritual ancestors. Rich and fruitful as the Bible is, it will not simply leap off the page and into our lives. Its view of the world and its concept of the world's story are already troublesome before we even climb onto the slippery slopes of theological language. But lest we despair of getting anything out of the thicket of words in the Bible, please keep in mind that our object is not just the Bible but the God who stands behind it and speaks through it. Like love, the encounter with God is through the medium of words and enriched by our deeper understanding of the meaning of those words. But the encounter itself, like true love, is much more than words.

That encounter does not happen when we simply pick up old stories and lay them uncritically atop modern ones. The God we meet in scripture is consistent in expectation but wondrously different in application. The real trick is to approach the Bible expectantly, as one would approach an ancient meeting ground, listening for the voice of the One to be met there. And the experience of faithful people through the centuries is that the God who comes to meet us steps into our finite world of time and place with a wisdom that fits our time and our place.

Mere readers of the Bible can find almost anything they want to find in scripture; those who *listen* to the Bible—who hear, read, mark, learn, and inwardly digest its words, who know the Lord's voice—can experience the grace of God. That is obviously a more challenging enterprise than finding a verse from the Bible that seems to endorse what we already want to do. In the next chapter I will consider ways to approach and meet that challenge, but for now it is enough to be aware that alongside the many obstacles our world places between us and scripture, the Bible itself is tricky and requires something more than simple research. A little time with a concordance or some other tool will undoubtedly provide us with the words we want to hear, but it takes a particular kind of faith to hear what we need to hear.

---

two stories

Rather than develop that kind of listening in theory, let me introduce you to some people who went to the meeting ground, listened, and followed, in their own unique ways.

Oscar Romero was born in 1917 in tiny Ciudad Barrio in southern El Salvador, entered seminary at the age of seven, and quickly adapted to living under the authority of the church. That conformity, coupled with his disciplined heart and brilliant mind, propelled him to the Gregorian University in Rome. When his studies were completed, Romero returned to El Salvador to begin his predictable and steady rise in the church bureaucracy: secretary for the diocese, cathedral canon, secretary for the National Conference of Bishops, church newspaper editor, and seminary professor. The needs of the world around him never quite caught his eye. In the 1950s, when 60 percent of the land in El Salvador was owned by 2 percent of the people, fourteen families controlled 50 percent of the national wealth, and death squads moved with impunity through the night, Romero maintained that the greatest concern for the church was "spiritualizing the clergy." He was the darling of the status quo, the kind of person that ruling elites like to reward with high office.

By 1977 he was Archbishop of El Salvador—and he found himself in the meeting ground. After fifty years of reading scripture, Romero finally heard the Word of the Lord. As Amos wrote seventeen hundred years before, "The lion has roared; who will not fear? The Lord GOD has spoken; who can but prophesy?" (3:8). Accordingly, he went to conduct the funeral of a priest friend, Father Rutilio Grande, who had been murdered for criticizing the wealthy, and the compliant bishop who went to Grande's funeral never returned. The new Oscar Romero wrote, "A church that does not unite itself with the poor in order to denounce from the place of the poor the injustice committed against them is not truly the Church of Jesus Christ." It put him in harm's way, but he declared, "How sad it would be in a country where such horrible murders are being committed if there were no priests among the victims." He took Christ's way of reconciliation to heart when he reminded the members of death squads that "the peasants you kill are your brothers and sisters." And eventually those death squad members came for him, gunning him down as he celebrated the Eucharist at the altar. The old Romero earned the patronizing pats of the elite. The new Romero earned a bullet through the heart and the crown of life.

Oscar Romero's story need not set us off on the road to martyrdom, but it does tell us something about meeting God. The bishop had heard the Word of God over and over. He knew that God has a peculiar and consistent attachment to the lame, the least, and the lost. He had heard it in God's care for murderous Cain and enslaved Israel as well as in laws about the rights of sojourners and meeting the needs of widows and orphans. As a learned theologian he had ancient and sophisticated words for God's peculiar preoccupation with the weak, but it had never occurred to him that it should become Oscar Romero's preoccupation as well. He had sung the *Magnificat* ten thousand times, and knew the words by heart: "He hath showed strength with his arm; he hath scattered the proud in the imagination of their hearts. He hath put down the mighty from their seat, and hath exalted the humble and meek. He hath filled the hungry with good things, and the rich he hath sent empty away." But it had always been the music of praise, never a plan of action. Every Maundy Thursday he had ritually obeyed the command to wash one another's feet. It was good liturgy, but then it began to point toward good living. He had been in the midst of the words of scripture but had never opened his eyes to meet the living Word that is in them. He had gone to the meeting ground again and again and never connected it to the world in which he lived. His friend's death brought the world and the Word close enough together for him to see the energy of God's love connecting them. It changed everything. Such is the power of the meeting ground to which each of us is invited to go, with Bible in hand.

The second story of the Bible's power is that of a person who lived in a place and time quite different from Oscar Romero's. In 1797, before Americans had begun to hear the full implications of the six-year-old Bill of Rights, a slave girl was born in New York's Hudson Valley. She was given the name Isabella and was fortunate enough to be raised to the age of nine by her parents. Her mother was a woman of deep faith who taught her daughter that only God could assist and guide them through the pain of their enslavement. Mother and daughter were illiterate but possessed the words of scripture in the same manner as the earliest believers, by rote.

In 1806 Isabella was sold off, like her nine siblings had been before her, separated from everything that was familiar and committed to a series of owners, cruelties, and humiliations. Her body bore the scars of numerous beatings and injuries. Hardship drives people in a variety of directions. Some become cynical and bitter, others sink into despair, while many seek vengeance. Isabella was, like her mother, driven to a seemingly inexhaustible hope.

In 1826, a year before emancipation came to New York, Isabella "stole herself" as the saying goes. She was always quick to point out that she did not run away, as that would have been "wicked," violating the biblical admonition that slaves obey their masters. She "walked off," which she regarded as more acceptable. What she walked into was the ferment historians call the Great Awakening, a time of unprecedented evangelical vigor and power. She was led to the first kind white family she had known, the Van Wegeners, and to the Methodist Church, in which she was "overwhelmed with the greatness of the Divine Presence." Her deep and hopeful faith found confirmation in community and a continuing conversation with that "Divine Presence." "I talk to God and God talks to me," she said.

She spent several years in various utopian communities popular at the time but finally set out to join the swelling ranks of itinerant preachers who were carrying the gospel message from camp meetings to crossroads. This vast, unorganized, and mostly uneducated throng shared the spirit of Saint Francis in taking the missionary charges of

Jesus in literal ways. They traveled the countryside and, in Isabella's case, spoke in cities. At the beginning of her preaching ministry in 1843, so the story goes, she stopped to ask for a drink of water at a farmer's well. She was asked her name and decided on the spot that she would be called by what she was rather than by the old slave name. "Sojourner," she answered. She was asked her last name and, as in the slave days, gave the name of her new master, Truth.

So it was that Sojourner Truth stepped onto the world's stage. Her six-foot height, deep and resonant voice, sweeping gestures, and powerful faith helped her to be one of those "slaves who could not read [but] became renowned for their ability to infuse ordinary existence with profound spiritual meaning."[3] Her first priority was freeing the enslaved and helping those whose freedom was new. That ministry brought her into contact and collaboration with Frederick Douglass, whom she once chided for being too negative; Harriet Beecher Stowe, who added to Sojourner's fame with a widely read article calling her a voice of God; and Abraham Lincoln, who posed with her in what became a famous picture.

Where did your Christ come from? From God and a woman! Man had nothing to do with Him. If the first woman God ever made was strong enough to turn the world upside down all alone, these women together ought to be able to turn it back, and get it right side up again! And now they is asking to do it, the men better let them. — *Sojourner Truth*

But Sojourner was to find out what many others, including the Roman Catholic radical Dorothy Day and the Baptist preacher Martin Luther King, Jr., learned. The Bible, when taken seriously, does not allow us to stick to one truth, one message, or a single proclamation. Whereas Dorothy Day felt compelled by scripture to take an unpopular pacifist position during the 1940s "Good

War," and Martin Luther King was led to condemn the war in Vietnam alongside his affirmation of civil rights, Sojourner found herself a champion of women's rights before the issue of slavery had been resolved and long before the issues of racism were even recognized.

One can get a flavor of her fire from what is probably her most famous speech, given extemporaneously at a women's rights meeting in Akron, Ohio, in 1851. After hearing a series of male clergy insist that women are the weaker sex more in need of masculine care than of human rights, Sojourner could take it no more. According to one eyewitness she pointed at one of the speakers and thundered:

> That man over there says that women need to be helped into carriages, and lifted over ditches, and to have the best place everywhere. Nobody ever helps me into carriages, or over mud-puddles, or gives me any best place! And ain't I a woman? Look at me! Look at my arm! I have ploughed and planted, and gathered into barns, and no man could head me! And ain't I a woman? . . . I have borne thirteen children, and seen most all sold off to slavery, and when I cried out with my mother's grief, none but Jesus heard me! And ain't I a woman? . . . What's [intellect] got to do with women's rights or negroes' rights? If my cup won't hold but a pint, and yours holds a quart, wouldn't you be mean not to let me have my little half measure full? [4]

She was a David with only one smooth stone as she faced a multitude of Goliaths. That stone was the God she met in the Bible she could not read. And the Goliaths fell, one by one.

why change?

The Word of the Lord takes different forms. The Bible is one of them and Jesus, "the Word made flesh," is another. There is a well-known story recorded in the gospel of John in which people are deserting Jesus because of his preaching. He asks his disciples if they want to leave as well, and Peter replies, "Lord, to whom can we go? You have the words of eternal life" (John 6:68). What was true of Jesus, the living Word, is also true of the Bible, the printed word. Where else would we go? It has a unique place in the relationship of God and God's people, a place that is not completely filled by any other. It is where our spiritual ancestors and our contemporaries have returned over and over because it has the words of eternal life.

Yet in every age those words are difficult to understand and keep in focus. Episcopalians probably deserve the label "biblical illiterates," and there are many reasons for this. Some may be found in the world we live in, many are in the Bible itself, and more than a few can be traced to our own sinfulness in failing to make what William James called a proper "connection with the higher powers." We are a people in need of what God is offering us in the Bible—the meeting ground where we can make that connection. But how we approach the Bible does not enable us to draw fully on its resources and experience its power, while the shifting world around us makes the task harder, not easier. That is why we need to reorient and transform the way we do things, and that is what we will be exploring in the next chapters.

Lest we enter this journey with a sense of futility, let's take a moment to remember how the Bible became the Bible. It is important to remember that the books of the Bible were chosen as sources of divine authority in times of enormous dislocation and change, in places where people were facing uncertainty, exile, and tragedy. They were trying to interpret their individual and community experience, face an uncertain future, or sort out right and wrong belief. Not every ancient piece of writing was included in the canon, and the texts that earned their place in the canon did so for various reasons. Some bore the name of prophets like Moses, Samuel, and Isaiah; others resided in the Temple and thus were thought to possess spiritual authority; and still others were approved by religious leaders. These scriptures are the distillation of two hundred generations of faithful living, or at least the struggle to be faithful. But as you might imagine, not everyone found the same value in the same sources. There had to be some decision by people in authority as to which texts were in and which were out; otherwise your Bible might omit Leviticus and include the Chronicles of Narnia because you don't get much from the first but really like the second. So the decisions as to which books ultimately make up the Bible involved a community of leaders evaluating the books' authority and sacred character.

Understanding how those choices were made can be instructive for us, too, because it was the absence of certainty and the difficulty of knowing how to proceed that led religious leaders to settle on these books. It is generally thought that the Pentateuch and some of the major historical books entered the canon at a time of crisis in the sixth century BCE, when the Babylonians conquered Jerusalem, destroyed the Temple, and sent the people of Israel off into exile. These first books helped the exiles know how they might sing the Lord's song "in a strange land." When the exiles returned fifty years later at the time of Ezra and Nehemiah, they faced the daunting task of rebuilding their city walls as well as the deeper task of figuring out what exactly their defeat and exile had meant. That search for understanding led to the next round of decisions about the canon, which grew to include the prophetic books. In 70 CE another tragedy struck as the Romans destroyed the Second Temple and the entire priestly and cultic system that had grown up around it. One of the last acts of the Temple authorities was to designate The Writings (Psalms, Proverbs, and other wisdom literature in the Hebrew scriptures) as part of the canon, to enable a dispersed people to know what they could rely on when the traditional religious systems could no longer guide them.

The books we accept as the New Testament were similarly chosen in a series of church councils in response to other kinds of serious problems. When the new Christian communities began to take their place in the Greco-Roman world, they came upon some very urbane and sophisticated ways of thinking that threatened to undermine the gospel as they understood it. For Greek philosophers, matter was inherently evil and spirit was good. Therefore the idea of the Word (in Greek, the *logos*) becoming flesh was so offensive they maintained that Jesus was not really human but only looked that way. Gnostic dualism—the view that good and evil are equal contenders in a struggle for the world—was a threat to the monotheism of the Judeo-Christian tradition. It was against the background of theological struggle with Gnostics and Arians that the New Testament canon came into being—and why the gospel of Mark and letters of Paul remained, while other early Christian writings were discarded.

This quick sketch of how the Bible came to be reveals that our ancestors chose these books to guide them and help form identity in tumultuous and confusing times. Today the forces of globalization and immigration are redrawing the map of our world just as dramatically as the *Pax Romana* reconceived the ancient world. New and confusing understandings of life flow freely; postmodernism edits the flash cards we have always used to study and understand life. The structures of faith communities are changing as megachurch, cyberchurch, virtual church, and emerging church become an overshadowing presence next to the traditional parish church. The old mainline denominations are being pushed to the sidelines by increasingly secular and interfaith realities. Our era is as full of uncertainty as the times of our ancestors who hiked into Babylon, stood in the ruins of the Temple, or carried an untested gospel into a sophisticated Greek world. The Bible has stood the test of troubled and troubling times because it was designed for such times. The Episcopal Church is in a perfect position to draw on the ancient truths of scripture to guide us through the uncharted waters of the twenty-first century, and we can expect those truths to be the place where we meet the Lord just as we have for generations.

chapter two

The Art of Effective Bible Study

Some years ago I was involved in a Bible study that included several local clergy as well as lay members of our congregations. The focus of the study was the lessons for the coming Sunday. The point was to help the clergy prepare for the sermon we each had to deliver on the texts, and it was a valuable and enjoyable way to begin the week. One of the best lessons I learned came from a layman named John, who worked at a truck weighing station on the interstate highway. As usual, we clergy were much involved in a certain text—going deeper and deeper into it, parsing words, splitting hairs, and exercising our academic muscles. Suddenly John stopped us in our tracks by exclaiming loudly, "Trucks!" We asked what he meant. "I weigh trucks," he said. "What has all of this got to do with weighing trucks?" In the embarrassed silence that followed, it became obvious that we had lost the essential connection to real lives that makes the Bible so powerful and relevant.

The Archbishop of Canterbury, Rowan Williams, tells us that for the Bible to do what it is intended to do there must be a connection between what he calls "the world in front of the text," meaning the communities for which the words were originally written and the far different communities in which we find ourselves today. Without that connection scripture becomes "rootless," either dominated by one world or the other.[5] Our little group had followed a well-worn path into this trap; we were lost *in* one world and lost *to* the other. We failed to remember that what God was saying to the original hearers of the text will be consistent with what God has to say to us in our own time. Finding that connection is the heart and the art of effective Bible study (to say nothing of good preaching). It is what makes a meeting ground out of an ancient text.

In this chapter I will explore the principles we Episcopalians can apply in becoming better readers of the Bible through seeking that connection. I will look at where these principles come from and at how they have been successfully applied. The central point is that we do not need new principles for transformation as much as we need a return to the original ones.

the Anglican way

Anglican tradition has given us a tried-and-true way to study and understand scripture. There are distinctions to be made, of course, among the ways that Roman Catholic, Pentecostal, Eastern Orthodox, Baptist, and Anglican Christians listen to God's Word. Those distinctions do not require us to make judgments that would label them as right or wrong or even better or worse. The Bible, like most things in life, can be profitably approached in a variety of ways. My purpose will be to explore that particular Anglican way and demonstrate that it is a valuable, fruitful, and compelling method for hearing and being touched by God's Word.

Our particular approach to scripture grew out of our common Judeo-Christian heritage and took a specific turn during the English Reformation. Shaped, like the Bible itself, in a time of uncertainty and strife, the Anglican approach is uniquely suited to serve us in such times. It gives central place to scripture but knows that God speaks to us through many mediums. It knows that hearing the Word of God requires a serious sifting through the many words of the printed Bible as well as through the many factors that both inform and cloud our view of our world.

Anglicans understand that the Bible is a meeting ground and must keep both eye and ear on the One we find there. Our approach to scripture is a path that has been well-used by God and the people of God for centuries. This is not to deny that it has also been misused in ways that run counter to the interests of God and the bringing in of God's kingdom: good people with solid learning and pure intent have drawn some very destructive conclusions from the Bible, as have others with little knowledge and bad intentions. No methodology, including ours, is immune to these dangers. Anglicanism has traditionally relied on the leading of the Spirit and the discernment of the Christian community to keep us on track. In addition, we have developed a healthy respect for the kind of uncertainty that leaves us open to correction, discovery, and guidance without paralyzing us into inaction. We know that we follow Christ across rough terrain and that we often stumble. Our best instincts are to rejoice in our bruises if we have in fact stumbled over new and greater truth.

There is a wonderful story behind the emergence of our Anglican way of understanding scripture that begins in the deep roots of our common heritage. The first lesson we learn from the Judeo-Christian approach to scripture is that people should go to the Bible as a matter of *routine*. You will recall the story in the gospels about Jesus going to the synagogue in Nazareth, where he read from the prophet Isaiah, for Sabbath worship "as was his custom." That story marks the beginning of Jesus' public ministry and has great implications for our understanding of it, but the story also reminds us that reading scripture was a routine part of corporate worship and village life in Israel. Our ancestors knew that the Bible was not like the oracles of the pagan world, to which people turned only in times of crises to receive guidance. Our faith has always spoken of a *relationship* with God. Relationships, whether with friends or with God, are sustained by regular, routine, and repeated contact. The Bible is not and never has been something we keep behind a glass we only break in case of emergency.

That basic truth of Judaism was taken up and affirmed in the monastic communities of the Christian church. Many of the early monastic rules included the discipline of *lectio divina* or "divine reading," a discipline that is still widely practiced today. It refers to a four-part process of slow, contemplative, and prayerful reading of scripture through studying, pondering, listening, and praying from God's Word—a method that allows us to hear God's voice. When Saint Benedict of Nursia laid the foundations for monastic life in Europe in the early sixth century he enshrined this approach in the daily rhythms of his rule. I will address *lectio divina* and other methods more fully in the next chapter, but for now let us simply note that one of the first messages of our common Judeo-Christian tradition is that the Bible is not an owner's manual that we turn to only when something breaks down. It is to be read regularly because it is about relationship and not merely repair.

A second basic principle we can see at work in our common heritage is that the Bible is a treasure of great power that is to be approached respectfully and expectantly. The central importance of scripture in the Judeo-Christian tradition is one measure of the respect in which it is held. The manifestations of its power in people's lives (and the attempts of those in authority to control it) are the reasons we can continue to approach it with high expectations, anticipating the meeting that moves lives. Thomas Cranmer, the sixteenth-century Archbishop of Canterbury and chief architect of the Book of Common Prayer, saw that the daily Bible reading routine of the monasteries had enormous value in developing and strengthening spiritual life, but he also knew that ordinary people could not maintain the cloister's rigorous schedule of worship and study. Cranmer's solution was to design a manageable routine of daily reading and prayer through the services of Matins and Vespers—what we now know as Morning and Evening Prayer. It is through routines like these that people do experience the living God and know their lives to be deepened, empowered, and enriched in the process.

It may plainly appear by the common prayers in the Church...that all the whole Bible (or the greatest part thereof) should be read over once in the year, intending thereby, that the Clergy...should (by often reading, and meditation of God's word) be stirred up to godliness themselves, and be more able to exhort others by wholesome doctrine.... And further, that the people (by daily hearing of holy Scripture read aloud in Church) should continually profit more and more in the knowledge of God, and be the more inflamed with the love of his true religion. *—Preface to the First Book of Common Prayer (1549)*

This intense veneration for scripture is also seen in the work of the early monasteries, as they copied and protected the biblical texts and, at the same time, rejoiced in them. Many men and women were drawn to monastic life as a refuge from the confusion that followed the collapse of the Roman Empire and the disintegration of its system of laws and customs. An enormous amount of time and energy went into copying biblical texts—as well as decorating and embellishing the pages. The Irish *Book of Kells* is probably the most famous of these illuminated manuscripts, but there are many examples of both serious symbolism and wry whimsy festooning the words of scripture. Since we have been thinking of the Bible as a meeting ground, consider that the scribes of the early years chose to decorate that ground with all manner of art as a celebration of its importance in their lives and in life itself. Of course greed and avarice had their place—when Saint Columba left his native Ireland in the sixth century to establish the community of Iona, his reason for going on this journey was not only missionary zeal, but also because he was on the losing side in a bloody feud over possession of a copy of the Psalms! That our ancestors would value the scriptures is one thing; that they would kill each other to possess them is something else.

Even the architecture of church buildings helped to illustrate and teach the words and images of scripture. From the wall paintings of the early Roman churches and catacombs to the great icons of the Eastern churches, art has long been employed as a means of expressing the stories and truths of the Bible. In the great cathedrals of the Gothic period, walls were supported externally by buttresses, which left the walls themselves free and unencumbered. Stained-glass windows began to appear in a shower of multicolored light. In styles as creative and expressive as that of any medieval illuminator, these artisans told the biblical story in hues and symbols, images and tableaux available to all. The point is that our ancestors knew that the thing to do with the new art form was to share the biblical story because it was life's anchor and rudder, providing grounding and guidance in good times and bad. It was but one of the many indicators that the church knew the power of scripture.

It was not just the possession of these valuable texts (as in Columba's case), but the interpretation of them that brought out the worst in us. As Christianity spread throughout Europe, attempts to translate the Bible from Latin into the common language of the people were resisted with ruthless force by the church. As long as the texts were in Latin, only the clergy and educated lay leaders and rulers could understand them, and thus the interpretation of the Bible could be tightly controlled by those in power. Those few did all they could do, including torture and death, to keep the texts of the Bible out of the hands of the general population. That our ancestors would value the scriptures is one thing, that they would kill each other over copies of it is something else. Both the weeds and the wheat bear witness to the value of this book.

With the abundance of Bible translations readily available to us today, we can lose sight of the power of the scriptures, and in our familiarity can fail to give the Bible the respect it deserves. We can also take the gift of hearing or reading the Bible in our common language for granted, and forget to come to the Bible expectantly. The Bible still startles, comforts, guides, challenges, and changes lives. My first experience with the power of the scriptures was when I was thirteen and accepted a scholarship from the churches in our region to go to church camp. I did not realize until later that accepting the scholarship required me to read a lesson in the Fall Convocation joint worship service—my first before such a large gathering! My sense of anxiety had reached the early stages of panic as the dreaded day approached. When I arrived at the service I was told to read Psalm 27, which begins with these words: "The LORD is my light and my salvation; whom then shall

I fear? The LORD is the strength of my life; of whom then shall I be afraid?" I immediately realized the truth of the words and the shallowness of my fears. Was the text coincidence? Maybe. Was it God's Word speaking and setting my fears aside? Definitely! I had the distinct feeling that something, maybe Someone, was speaking to me through those words. It is a feeling I have had many times over in subsequent years.

> All I know is that when I pray coincidences happen, and when I do not pray coincidences do not happen.
> — *Archbishop William Temple*

In that very minor moment in human history, I was surprised to hear the word I needed and had not been able to work out on my own. With it I took my place, well back in the corner but still on the same stage, with predecessors like Sojourner Truth and Oscar Romero. In its own way, it was the same kind of revelation Francis of Assisi received when he heard the gospel directive to "go, sell what you own, and give the money to the poor," and as he did so he embarked on an entirely new way of life. It was of the same substance, if not the same scope, as the moment when Martin Luther realized the truth of Saint Paul's words that we are "saved by grace through faith" rather than through our own efforts, thus giving rise to a profound reformation of the church's practices and teachings. It was a tiny fraction of what happened when Americans heard Martin Luther King, Jr., quote the words of the prophet Amos, "let justice roll down like waters, and righteousness like an ever-flowing stream"—after which the civil rights movement became unstoppable. It was much closer to the countless times millions of people have received comfort in the words of the Twenty-third Psalm, or have been awed by hearing the Beatitudes, or have changed their behavior because of the influence of the Ten Commandments.

My first Bible was the King James Version. It had a zipper, and the words of Jesus were in red. Perhaps you had one or have seen one like it. Its language is regal and inspiring as no other I have ever known. I do not read it as often anymore because subsequent developments in scholarship and in the usages of modern English have allowed translators to come much closer to connecting the original Hebrew and Greek meanings with the contemporary mind. But the reasons for the King James Version, its methodology if you will, remain at the heart of our church's way of approaching the Bible in any translation.

The pre-Reformation English church resisted any attempts to translate the Bible from the Latin Vulgate into the language of the English people. We can see the enormous desire on the part of its leaders to protect and control the text through the story of William Tyndale, a cleric and gifted linguist who in the 1520s was determined to make the Bible available to the common people. John Foxe's *Book of Martyrs* reports (it may be apocryphal) a heated exchange with a prominent English clergyman in which Tyndale cried out, "I defy the Pope, and all his laws; and if God spares my life, I will cause the boy that drives the plow in England to know more of the scriptures than the Pope himself." He went into hiding after the completion of his New Testament, and was put to death for heresy in 1536. Nonetheless, Tyndale's translation went on to have a far-reaching influence on the Bible translations of the Reformation, including the Great Bible of 1539, the Geneva Bible of 1560, the Bishops' Bible of 1568, the Douay-Rheims Bible of 1582–1609, and the King James Version of 1611.

After the death of Elizabeth I in 1603, her successor, James I, was persuaded by the Puritan party to commission a new translation of the Bible. Their motivation was to level the playing field between the Puritan's favorite translation, the Geneva Bible, and the Church of England's Bishop's Bible. The matter was not trivial, as the two versions presented different viewpoints and distinct theological interpretations. The Geneva Bible was full of footnotes and cross-references that supported the strict Calvinist views of the Puritans, whereas the Bishop's Bible had been put forward as a rebuttal to this Protestant influence and was the only text allowed in English churches. Once again the polarizing instincts of faith set up an either-or situation.

James, a clever man who knew his way around church politics as well as theology, called a conference at Hampton Court to discuss the issues between conservative Puritans and the more liberal factions of the Church of England. On hearing the Puritans complain of the corruption of those versions used in English churches, the king agreed but then replied that out of all the translations the Geneva Bible was the worst. The conference therefore resolved "that a translation be made of the whole Bible, as consonant as can be to the original Hebrew and Greek; and this to be set out and printed, *without any marginal notes* [italics added], and only to be used in all churches of England in time of divine service." The resulting King James Version of the Bible attempted to take a middle course between these two extremes. The scholar-translators were told to dig deeply into the original texts in order to let the Bible speak for itself and let the people understand for themselves. This position, which brought us one of the greatest works of literature, scholarship, and faith in English, couples the ancient Judeo-Christian respect for scripture with the expectation that God would use it for God's own purposes.

The theologian Richard Hooker was not part of the making of the King James Version of the Bible but its composition well represented his heart and mind. It is to Hooker's understanding of scripture, its authority and interpretation that we will turn next.

Richard Hooker was born into a merchant family in Exeter in 1554. His mentor during his student days was John Jewel, Bishop of Salisbury, who did much to hammer out the distinctiveness of the Church of England against Roman Catholicism. Blessed with a marvelously keen mind, Hooker settled into teaching Hebrew at Oxford until the age of twenty-nine, when he became Master of the Temple (referring to Temple Church on Fleet Street in London). It was a prestigious six-year assignment that sharpened Hooker's thinking and molded his character. Fleet Street was the gathering place for lawyers and magistrates; in an age when church and state were as inseparable as bone and marrow, lawyers and clerics had much to say to one another.

When Hooker took up his position, the Thirty-nine Articles formally articulating the unique position of the Church of England on the theological landscape had been a fixture for over twenty years. The full implications of those articles, however, were far from clear. The business of law and lawyers is to apply the core legal documents of a society to day-to-day living. The business of theology and preachers is to do the same with core religious documents. The Temple Church on Fleet Street, where civil law and church doctrine enjoyed a nearly seamless relationship, was the perfect place for the right person to make a great difference. It was a bit like becoming chaplain to the Supreme Court.

Hooker was not a great preacher in the dramatic sense. His nearsightedness kept his head bowed over the reading stand and his weak voice was not supported by either gesture or inflection. His sermons must have required a great deal of effort on the part of those in the pew, but in a time of theological and doctrinal warfare he was generous toward his opponents, including John Calvin. He took the Puritans to task with gusto, but avoided the kind of recriminatory language that characterized his age, even while making his own case abundantly clear. The spirit of tolerance, forbearance, and inclusion that we Episcopalians most like about ourselves can be traced to the heart of Hooker. It allows us, among other things, to let the Bible speak differently to different people in different times. We are not overly burdened with a need to pass judgment on the biblical methodology or even the theological interpretations of others. Richard Hooker did not create this attitude of comprehensiveness, nor did he embody it in a unique manner. He did, however, enshrine it at the center of our identity.

Hooker was content with mystery and had no need to spell out the details of theology or religious experience. When we speak of the Bible as a meeting ground that we approach respectfully and expectantly, aware of the mystery of encounter with God, we are following his path. Wonder and expectation remain the final words in our biblical methodology because we have found that we are able to hear God more richly and abundantly in that attitude of openness than with a strict formula or a set of approved interpretations.

After six years at Temple Church, Hooker requested assignment to a rural parish near Canterbury, where he could devote time to writing. The result was *Treatise on the Laws of Ecclesiastical Polity*, an eight-volume work that has done much to determine the thinking of our particular tradition. There are many astute treatments of *Ecclesiastical Polity* that make clear our indebtedness to Richard Hooker. Our purposes are more narrow here, so I will only share with you something of the path he took among the myriad ways of understanding the Bible's authority that helped to draw the battle lines of sixteenth-century Europe.

The classical humanists of the day, such as Erasmus of Rotterdam, were intent on uncovering the historical texts and the original Greek and Hebrew manuscripts of the Bible. They viewed the Bible as one among many ancient texts and did not consider it to be inspired. Puritans, on the other hand, took the position that the Bible was the only source of real knowledge of God and salvation, and that what the Bible did not explicitly require of Christians must be forbidden. (This explains their attitude toward the sacraments and church ceremonies not found in scripture.) The mainstream of emerging Protestantism took a more permissive view; it affirmed the unique authority of the Bible but maintained that what was not expressly forbidden could be allowed. The Roman Catholic Council of Trent held still another view, that tradition shared equal authority with scripture, the Latin Vulgate was the only authorized version of the Bible, and that the Pope and his cardinals alone could provide the proper interpretation of it. Over the years these positions have certainly been modified, but this is a reasonable description of the theological landscape through which Hooker made his way.

So what was Hooker's point of view that has so influenced Anglicanism since his day? First, Hooker concurred that of course the Bible is central to the Christian faith and contains all things necessary to salvation (one of the best-known points of the Thirty-nine Articles). But he also agreed with the humanists in thinking that God's revelation comes through many avenues besides scripture. With this, Hooker departed from many "mainline" Protestants whose mantra was *sola scriptura* or "scripture alone," meaning that scripture is the sole arbiter of faith. Instead, Hooker believed that God is also revealed in the discoveries of science, in reflection on human experience, and in literature both sacred and secular.

Second, Hooker thought that the Roman Catholic Church was wrong to hold the interpretive reins of the Bible too tightly because the Spirit guides "all that are of God" through the faculty of reason. This God-given capacity is not just what one thinks or feels or has experienced. It is the Spirit-guided ability to draw things together, to discern the whole that makes sense of the parts, to perceive the truth and reach for the courage to act on it.

> Unto the Word of God...we do not add reason as a supplement to any maim or defect therein, but as a necessary instrument without which we could not reap by the scripture's perfection that fruit and benefit which it yieldeth. — *Richard Hooker*

However, Hooker did not believe that the gift of human reason meant that any thinking person could find God's truth in scripture all by him/herself. The Puritan insistence that interpretation was a simple process called "bare reading" resulted in what Hooker termed "bare feeding": it missed the full "fruit and benefit which [scripture] yieldeth." The Puritan approach would come close to what we would today call "biblical literalism." The meaning of a text, as Hooker and our church today maintain, is not just lying on the surface for all to see and acknowledge. The richness of a text is more subtle, drawing its meaning from a variety of contexts (both past and present) that are available to be explored by humans. That exploration is best done as a continuation of the struggles, insights, and conclusions of those who have gone before us in faith. Tradition, the wisdom of the church throughout the ages, while not on a par with the Bible, has a vital role in interpreting Holy Scripture.

The result of Richard Hooker's thoughtful reconciling of the extreme positions of his day is an approach to scripture that relies on reason and tradition for the fullness of understanding. Hooker did *not* come up with the analogy of scripture, tradition, and reason as a three-legged stool, and unfortunately that popular concept has left Anglicans with the erroneous impression that all three are equal. Instead, he specifically rejected the notion that the traditions of the church were on an equal par with scripture, and he would never have considered that human reason in any form could trump divine revelation in the Bible. Scripture is the foundational authority, while tradition and reason are subordinate—they are aids to interpreting the Bible, not its equal nor its competitor. But—and this is important—none of the three stands alone. Scripture does not lend itself to "bare reading," nor does reason alone lead us to God, nor can tradition by itself tell the story. All three must be in dialog for the greater truths to emerge.

I do not know what Hooker would have made of the addition of "experience" to scripture, tradition, and reason, as we often see added today, because he understood experience to be an integral part of what he meant by "reason." Our experiences of life shape our understanding of God and our interpretation of scripture and tradition. This would have seemed too obvious to Hooker to merit a separate category. He might have said that God makes things happen in this world and much of it is shrouded in mystery, but our perception and understanding of those events, when interpreted by faith, are a source of revelation.

Again, this does not mean that experience "trumps" everything else, but that the dialog among scripture, tradition, and reason can be joined by experience. Each enriches the other and illumines the whole. None stands alone. This dialog does not work well when confined to the level of biblical "proof-texting" to support a single point of view—the faith journey that limits itself to the literal surface of the Bible or is bound to go no further than tradition has gone before is more of a walk around the block than the kind of pilgrimage to which we are called. By the same token, those who favor their own perception of events above all others are left with a very small god indeed. Either way leads us into the same trap my little Bible study group fell into, missing the essential connection between the past and the present. The conversation works best when the deeper rhythms and wider truths of the Bible are allowed to speak to the experiences of life.

So what have we learned from this brief survey of the Anglican approach to scripture? First, we have a method that is grounded in the Judeo-Christian tradition of spending regular, respectful, and expectant time with the Bible, whether it be the use of *lectio divina* in Bible study or hearing the scriptures read during Sunday worship, or the daily offices. Second, in our emphasis on scripture, reason, and tradition we have a discipline of studying both the texts themselves and their interpretation by our forebears and our contemporaries, as well as of listening for the Spirit to inform and guide our powers of reasoning.

trusting the Spirit

What we do not have is a central authoritative person or persons to tell us the right answers. Lutherans have Luther, Presbyterians have Calvin, Roman Catholics have the Vatican, but Anglicans have a methodology that leaves ultimate responsibility with the reader. We do not have our own confessional statement beyond the Nicene and Apostles' Creeds we recite regularly in worship. The closest we have ever come to defining our faith is known as the Chicago-Lambeth Quadrilateral, which was written in the late nineteenth century to guide us in the new endeavors of what we now call ecumenism. It reminds us that the Bible, the traditional creeds, the major sacraments of baptism and Eucharist, and the role of bishops are central to our tradition. It is remarkable for its lack of dogmatic clarity. The point is that our church has a process but not a product. We know how to approach the meeting ground, but we do not tell people what God will say to them when they get there.

For this reason, the Anglican way places the final decision-making power not in a church hierarchy but in individuals in community, which leads to complications of its own. It leaves us vulnerable to serious misunderstandings and understandable discomfort. Some critics say that because the Episcopal Church does not spell out or "set in stone" the results of our Bible study or how it applies to ethical situations, it does not matter what conclusions we reach. In other words, no one has the authority to tell us that we are wrong. There is some merit to this concern: it has been jokingly said that any sentence beginning with "Some Episcopalians believe..." will be accurate no matter how you finish it. We do have a tendency to hear what we want to hear from scripture—but it is worth noting that the various authorities, theologians, and hierarchies who tell others what the Bible is really saying are subject to the same tendencies. Still, it is a bit awkward when people ask what our church believes about this or that and we point to a way of thinking about the problem rather than giving a clear answer.

The position of the Episcopal Church on abortion is one example. Some denominations are abundantly clear about their rules on abortion, no matter what the circumstances. At the 1994 General Convention our church took a position that it has consistently reaffirmed and that illustrates an approach to moral issues that parallels our approach to scripture: we are told *how* to decide but not *what* to decide. The resolution (A054) clearly spells out the seriousness of the decision, affirms that it is the right and responsibility of the mother to make that decision, but requires that the decision be made prayerfully and with the "advice and counsel of members of the Christian community." This means that faithful Episcopalians can and do come to different conclusions about abortion. This is understandably offensive to some; to others, it is an exercise in the kind of freedom and responsibility that God has chosen to give us and part of what it means to be "made in the image of God." We prefer the struggle to be faithful in that "image" with its often frightening freedom to the sacrifices that conformity to a set of fixed conclusions requires. As King James would have his translation "without marginal notes," but trusting the Spirit to guide the reader, so we continue to trust the Spirit to guide the believer.

We are, of course, not free to come to any conclusion we want, and it does matter to Episcopalians what we believe. It matters a great deal that we conform to the revelations of scripture, its deeper rhythms and wider truths, not just its surface words. God's care for the lame, the least, and the lost, which is affirmed throughout the Bible, requires us first to do no harm and second to join in the works of healing and reconciliation. We must fit our lives and our actions within the boundaries of our faith, but the Bible, as well as all of salvation history, tells us that there is room for many faithful expressions within those boundaries. Living faithfully within those boundaries is not easy, however, because there is no authority to tell us that we are right. People want the assurance that their beliefs are as they should be, especially in times of uncertainty, and the confidence that comes from *knowing* they are right. This confidence is not easily come by in a system as open-ended as ours; for us the Bible is not a book of answers we can turn to like an owner's manual or a dictionary. And as difficult as it may be for us, faith includes an element of doubt as surely as courage includes fear and discipline includes effort. Faith is what we have when certainty is not possible.

The more subtle value is confidence, which is very different from certainty in its focus but much like it in its rewards. Certainty is centered in the individual; it is something you or I might possess. Confidence is rooted in someone else. Certainty would be nice but it is not really an option in a life of faith. Confidence gives us the courage to act on our beliefs without requiring the world around us to conform to those beliefs. Confidence can trust in the ongoing leading of the Spirit, knowing that God's truth is always full of potential and discovery; certainty in faith is a contradiction in terms.

In the Genesis story of creation we learn that all of life is good but that "it is not good" for human beings to be alone. This is the initial call to community based on God's knowledge that we need one another at many levels. One could say that the rest of the Bible is the story of God calling people into relationship with God and with one another. Ours is a community-based faith because healthy relationships with other people are required to keep our relationship with God on track in much the same way that tradition and reason are required to keep our reading of scripture on track. The "other people" of the Christian community include the sages who have gone before who have shaped the traditions that inform us; the contemporaries who challenge us with their differences from us; the loved ones who support us in common causes; the elders to whom we give respect; and the leaders to whom we owe allegiance. This community of faith is the repository of scripture, tradition, and reason, the interpreter of experience, the setting for the sacraments, and the home of our companions in the meeting ground where God is known. All of these things together enable us to be responsible for our own decisions because none of us need be alone in making them.

How can we know if we as a community of faith are on the right track? Jesus once said, "No good tree bears bad fruit, nor again does a bad tree bear good fruit; for each tree is known by its own fruit" (Luke 6:43–44). The point that we can know the value of something by the results it produces is a wise and fair standard to apply to our church's approach to scripture. The Anglican "tree" is rooted in the most ancient appreciations and disciplines of scripture. We branched out five hundred years ago to distinguish ourselves from the other fruit-bearing limbs of that tradition. We have faithfully stretched and grown in many ways. But what fruit have we borne? Is the fruit good, indicating that the tree is good? Or is it like another tree Jesus spoke of, one that has borne no fruit and is given one more chance before being cut down (Luke 13:6–9)?

The point of lay Bible study is to help lay people reclaim their authority as the People of God. — *Verna Dozier*

Many Episcopalians today would claim that our way of coming to scripture is wonderfully rich, and has indeed borne abundant fruit. Millions have followed our path to the meeting ground and have been deeply influenced in ways that allowed them to greatly influence others, from poets like John Donne, George Herbert, and T. S. Eliot to storytelling theologians like Dorothy Sayers, C. S. Lewis, and Madeleine L'Engle. Anglicans have borne the fruit of reform and martyrdom, prophetic witness, scholarship, and prayerful mysticism, as in the lives of people as diverse as F. D. Maurice and William Wilberforce, Desmond Tutu and Stephen Biko, Carter Heyward, Barbara Harris, David Pendleton Oakerhater, and Absalom Jones, Elizabeth Cady Stanton, Evelyn Underhill, Verna Dozier, and Esther de Waal, William Temple and Michael Ramsey, Marcus Borg and N. T. Wright.

All of these Anglicans and a host of others have followed the path from the earliest appreciations of scripture onto the trail blazed by Hooker and widened by many others to reach the meeting ground where they have heard the Word of the Lord. I do not intend to imply that our church's approach to scripture is unique in its ability to bear such fruit; my point is that, as we have seen, we come to scripture in a particular way and that way can be wonderfully rich. Can other paths do the same? Of course. Does this path "work" for everyone? Of course not. But it is our path and it works for us. This we know by the fruit that it has borne and continues to bear.

how does it work?

Our church has a method—a way, if you will—and it has borne much fruit. But how does it work? What is likely to happen if one were to follow this way to the meeting ground where countless brothers and sisters have met and heard the Lord? How is the connection made between the Bible lesson and the weighing of trucks—or whatever else makes up our daily lives? How does Rowan Williams's "world in front of the text" find its continuity with our world? While the answer is not as clear and detailed as the routines of an altar guild, we do know a good bit about it.

What takes place in scripture is called *theophany*, which literally means a manifestation of God. While we are always in the presence of God, we are not always aware of it. The occasions of such awareness are theophanies. You may be more familiar with the term *epiphany* since it is the name for one of our feast days in the church year. Epiphany means "manifestation," and while it is often associated with God's revealing, the word itself does not require that interpretation. Almost any discovery or sharing of oneself could be called an epiphany. Since we are talking specifically about meeting God, the best word is "theo-phany," or God revealed. In such moments two of the things we know about God come together.

The first is called transcendence, and refers to the unsearchable majesty of God. It comes to mind when we speak of God as Father. The visual arena of transcendence is "the vast expanse of interstellar space." It is what Isaiah experienced when he wrote of the Lord "high and lofty" and gave us the familiar "Holy, holy, holy is LORD of hosts; the whole earth is full of his glory" (6:3) The word "holy" means "separate," and since Isaiah did not have adjectives like super or colossal he gave emphasis by repeating the word. "Holy, holy, holy" means very holy, very separate, not like us at all. It is the reason Isaiah can also tell us that God's ways are not like our ways. That is what transcendence means.

The second attribute is God's immanence or nearness. It is what we experience as the work of God as Holy Spirit. It is what we reach for and rely on when we pray. When Moses asks the rhetorical question "What other great nation has a god so near to it as the LORD our God is whenever we call to him?" (Deuteronomy 4:7), or when Jesus tells us that God knows when a sparrow falls to the ground and can count the hairs on our head, they were both speaking of God's immanence.

In the Christian narrative these two realities come together most dramatically and completely in the Incarnation. Jesus is the transcendent Word become immanent flesh. Jesus is the ultimate theophany. But the holiness of God and the intimate care of God often come close enough in human experience for the energy of the two to arc like electricity between wires, illuminating our understanding and our lives. This is also theophany. Think of the story we call Jacob's ladder. The young man was totally, selfishly immersed in his own interests. His behavior had been so bad that he had to run away from the righteous anger of his brother and found himself in the desert with only a stone for a pillow. In that tiny frightened moment he had his experience of the majesty of God and could only say, "Surely the LORD is in this place—and I did not know it!... This is none other than the house of God, and this is the gate of heaven" (Genesis 28:16–17).

He said, "Go out and stand on the mountain before the LORD, for the LORD is about to pass by." Now there was a great wind, so strong that it was splitting mountains and breaking rocks in pieces before the LORD, but the LORD was not in the wind; and after the wind an earthquake, but the LORD was not in the earthquake; and after the earthquake a fire, but the LORD was not in the fire; and after the fire a sound of sheer silence. When Elijah heard it, he wrapped his face in his mantle and went out and stood at the entrance of the cave. Then there came a voice to him that said, "What are you doing here, Elijah?" (1 Kings 19:11–13)

Jacob's theophany raises an important point about the Word of God that is often overlooked and needs to be spelled out here. When God "speaks," the auditory moment is often bypassed. When you and I have a conversation, you say something, I listen to it, and on reflection come to a certain understanding of what you are trying to tell me. When we are in conversation with God, there is often no speaking or listening in the conventional sense. There is no auditory moment, when sound carries an idea from one brain to another. With God we usually discover that a new understanding has formed in our minds. Very few people actually hear a voice, but many have had this experience of realization that begins not with hearing but with having heard. Of course the Bible, as well as many faith stories outside of scripture, refers to people hearing God's "voice." I have no basis with which to challenge or rewrite those stories, but my guess is that if someone had been standing beside Moses with a tape recorder they would not have picked up any sound. I believe the dialog was real but its reality took place without auditory moments. Even dramatic theophanies like the time of Jesus' baptism, when we are told that a voice came from heaven proclaiming, "You are my Son, the Beloved; with you I am well pleased," do not necessarily have an auditory moment. The gospels do not tell us that everyone heard it, just that it was communicated. I believe it describes a moment of realization on Jesus' part, the moment when he recognized his unique relationship with God and role in life.

My point is not to change our understanding of theophanies in the Bible but to prepare us for our own meetings with God. We hold assumptions about people who hear voices that are very different from those of our ancestors. They could tell us of conversations with angels, demons, Satan, or God himself and see them as part of a continuing dialog with the supernatural. We tend to see such conversations as a manifestation of mental illness. I want us to be prepared for conversation with God because I believe that such conversation is not only possible but is continuous, if we have what Jesus called "the ears to hear." I do not believe that we should wait for an auditory moment when the ears on which we hang jewelry and glasses pick up a series of sound waves and send them to our brains for analysis. God's voice most often takes its root in our minds without troubling our auditory nerves. The "ears to hear" are in our minds and hearts, not on the side of our heads.

Because this kind of hearing is not as public and measurable as ordinary human conversation, it is vital that those who hear God check the message with the wider community. Hearing that takes place in our hearts and minds is subject to all of the distortion, self-interest, ignorance, and sin that dwell in our hearts and minds. One can never be sure if we have heard the voice of the Lord or something far less. That is why theophanies always need two hearings—one by an individual and then by the community around us. One reason it is not good to be alone, as the creation story tells us, but better to be in community is that when we are alone we often distort what we hear to suit our own interests. By ourselves we begin to worship ourselves. It is the community who keeps us honest.

Finally, one hallmark of theophany is that God always calls us into the future. The Creator of life is deeply committed to the direction of life, which never stops or runs backward. If God calls us to stop it is always to rest for the next step forward; the Good Shepherd continually keeps us moving along. Sometimes we are called to pause and turn inward to face what is inside of us; sometimes we are called to turn outward and face what is around us. But God always calls us forward.

We turn now to some of the contemporary expressions of our tradition that are available to us as we follow Christ into the unknown future.

Surveying the Methods

On July 20, 1969, Commander Neil Armstrong became the first man to set foot on the moon. His first words were dramatic—"That's one small step for man, one giant leap for mankind"—but his next were much more mundane and in touch with day-to-day living. "The surface is fine and powdery," he said. "I can kick it up loosely with my toe. It does adhere in fine layers, like powdered charcoal, to the sole and sides of my boots." The grand experience quickly turned to smaller, more manageable parts.

The contrast between the high drama of stepping onto the moon and the sticky dust of actually being there provides an introduction to this chapter. When faithful people enter the meeting ground of scripture they find themselves in a moment not unlike that of the astronaut. The God of Abraham, Isaac, and Jacob, the Lord who walked among us in Palestine, the Spirit that was poured out at Pentecost is at hand in a presence as awesome and mysterious as anything Commander Armstrong experienced. But that grand moment of mystery is made up of the simple acts of reading, marking, learning, and inwardly digesting a text. The means and manner in which we take those small steps make up the giant leap into the presence of God. Like the surface of the moon there are many pieces to bring together. Some are fine and powdery, some adhere in layers, some we can kick loosely, and some we may have to pry off, but all of them together make the tangible center of a great mystery.

After our general survey of the Anglican way of approaching the Bible in the previous chapter, in this chapter we will be considering some of the current practices in the Episcopal Church—the Bible studies that are making a difference in our lives today. It is not enough to know the grand plan we inherited from Richard Hooker and others without some insight into how they are being applied. Nor is it enough to develop a catalog of popular techniques and methods. If we are to consider the forces of transformation at work among us, we have to look at what makes an approach to scripture especially valuable for the future, just as our ancestors determined the canon of the Bible by asking what writings were best suited to address the unknown. In addition, as we continue to live into our relatively newfound commitment to diversity, we must learn how to learn from the groups making up that diversity. So we will want some understanding of the resources of value to the whole church that are being developed in the various parts of the church.

It is not my intention to provide a list of good and bad Bible study techniques. Such a list would be my personal judgment with little value outside of my personal experience of scripture. Telling people the "proper" way to read the Bible is like telling people the "right" way to choose a partner in marriage. There are far too many intangibles, most of which are beyond my knowing and none of my business. God is able to make divine conversation from many different elements, just as God is able to make happy marriages from many different people. However, just as there are some principles generally acknowledged as the basis for a successful marriage, there are also some fundamental things that can be said about successful Bible study. Exceptions abound in both categories, but that is no reason not to listen to what our experience as a church has to tell us.

Before we turn to these principles, however, we need to consider exactly what a Bible study method *is* and what it is *not*. Methods and systems for studying the Bible abound in the life of our church, but they play very different roles so it is important to know the difference. The word "method" comes from two Greek words: *meta,* which means "after" (as in following after), and *hodos,* which means "road" or "journey." A method is a way of proceeding. System comes from the Greek word *sustema,* which means "to gather together." Now before you start to roll your eyes and wonder what this has to do with anything, notice that methods are about motion, *moving* along a path; systems are about *taking a stand,* circling the wagons, staking out a position. In a method we know the path but not the answer we will find. In a system we know the answer and are showing the path by which one might come to it. The distinction is important because many people confuse the two, generally espousing a system as if it were a method.

For example, Archbishop Ndungane of South Africa hosted a very important and valuable conference for the Anglican Communion in March of 2007. The idea was to take steps Toward Effective Anglican Mission, TEAM for short. In his concluding remarks the Archbishop gave us a fine example of a system. "We will examine the Bible, the source of our mission, to speak against patriarchy and to advocate for equality. We will use scripture to combat domestic violence and sexual abuse." Few would argue against such a stand, nor can a serious student of scripture suggest that the Bible is disinterested in these goals. But neither does anyone suspect that the promised examination of the Bible will focus on Lot's decision to offer his virgin daughters to a lustful mob in Sodom and conclude that the abuse of women is occasionally sanctioned. The Archbishop knows the answer (domestic violence and sexual abuse are morally wrong) and is showing the biblical foundations for it. This is a very good thing, as we would not want our understanding of such important matters to be without a solid scriptural foundation. But it is a stand, not a path; a system, not a method.

A method, on the other hand, would lead us into the scriptures armed with questions rather than answers. It would help us to listen for the deeper rhythms of the Bible; to overhear the dialog between past and present, text and science, reason and revelation. The Benedictine discipline called *lectio divina* or holy reading is a method, pure and simple: read slowly, meditate, pray, contemplate. Notice how it differs from the system suggested at the TEAM Conference. Saint Benedict assumed neither a question nor an answer, but marked a path the faithful might follow. This method relies on a regular routine of holy reading, a gentle oscillation between exploring the kingdom of God and resting in it. This is the essence of a Bible study method.

Methods need not be as open-ended as *lectio divina*. Some of the most powerful experiences with scripture have been sharpened by questions or issues in the minds of readers. My first experience with hearing the Bible speak that I recounted earlier was made possible by the presenting issue of being afraid to read before a church full of strangers. When one reads the Bible with a question, decision, or situation in mind, the texts fairly bubble with insight and inspiration. As a preacher I have discovered what countless others have known: reading a text on Monday and having it in mind during the week allows the events of that week to be so deeply and profoundly interpreted by the text that the point of the sermon emerges with compelling clarity. It happens too subtly to be explained but too often to be doubted. Coming to scripture with a question or holding scripture up to a situation is an appropriate part of any method. Coming to scripture with a conclusion or interpretation already in mind is a part of a system. Ideally people create systems after using methods; that is, they come to a conclusion as a result of approaching the Bible openly. Theologies and positions taken in church conflicts that fall short of that ideal can easily be found, but naming them is, happily, beyond the scope of this book.

Bible study principles

In the Episcopal Church, a hallmark of Bible study will be an honoring of the principles our tradition has hewn and fashioned over the years, the points developed in the previous chapter:

+ Regular reading from throughout the canon of scripture keeps us from proof-texting.

+ An attitude of respect and expectation keep us open to the power of scripture.

+ Holding the Bible in dialog with tradition, reason, and experience protects us from the chaos of scripture's surface contradictions.

+ Reading the Bible in community makes it harder for us to impose our will on God's Word.

These are the basics that define our efforts as Episcopalians, the flags that tell who we are. Before we turn to particular Bible study methods we will look at these principles a bit more closely.

One of the best theologians in our church at the end of the nineteenth century was William Porcher DuBose, who taught at the University of the South and was instrumental in establishing the Episcopal seminary there. He was primarily a man of the Bible, one who understood its power and its problems. He once wrote that one of the Bible's "embarrassments" is that "we are attempting to address the world today, in the matter of its profoundest interest, in terms of the world two thousand years ago."[6] The difficulty of that task is the cause of Archbishop Rowan Williams's lament about "rootless" interpretations of scripture that do not engage the "the world in front of the text." Williams and DuBose know well the temptation to avoid the struggle of bridging the gap between the modern reader and the ancient writer. The Archbishop is clear in his concern that too many modern readers are "dominated by the time we think we occupy so that anything coming at us through an alien text is likely to be processed into whatever concerns us most."[7] It is a serious threat to the vitality of our relationship with God.

As listeners [to scripture], our primary responsibility is to receive.... But it remains true that this level of reading cannot happen if we are dominated by the time we think we occupy, so that anything coming at us through an alien text is likely to be processed into whatever concerns us now and subjected to the criteria by which we judge something as useful or useless for the time of our plans and projects. — *Rowan Williams*

Such modernism furrows the brows of our teachers and leaders, as well it should. Those of us whose place in the church is a little further back in the pack are also aware of the danger of the opposite, which we might call "ancientism." Few of us have escaped the sermon or Bible study that never emerges from the "world in front of the text." We have all sat through presentations that unpacked the ancient roots of words, described the customs of Greece, Rome, or Jerusalem, and connected one verse to another but never made any connection with matters of our dimmest, much less our profoundest, interest. Dense presentations that drive the faithful from expectation to disappointment to grim despair are at least as prevalent as shallow modern theories, and may be an even greater threat to our future. Among the miracles of the twentieth-century church was its consistent ability to make the gospel dull. It is the biblical equivalent of turning wine back into water, and it has done us every bit as much harm as trendy theologies. If the Episcopal Church expects scripture to be at the core of its vitality in the coming years, we will have to avoid the perils of both modernism and ancientism, and actively seek to be touched by the power of God that arcs between them.

COMMUNITY

The creation story in Genesis tells us that after the six days of bringing the universe into existence, God pronounced it all to be not only good but "very, very good." Humanity is included in that judgment, so we can allow ourselves to believe that it is good to be you and it is good to be me. God made us so and crowns us with the opportunity to be in, as far as we know, a unique-among-creatures relationship with God. We are given the Garden of Eden, with responsibilities, choices, and consequences that are not extended to others. The story goes on to tell us that after the sabbath rest, God took another look at us and made the first adjustment to the natural order of things. God observed that it was "not good that the man [*adam,* a Semitic word that means "people," referring to all of us] should be alone" (Genesis 2:18). The "adjustment" is, of course, Eve—a word that means "source," referring to birth-givers. Our ancestors were explaining in their own way the origin of families and in so doing they laid out the basic importance of all human relationships. It is not good for us to be alone, isolated. Such a condition does not threaten our goodness in God's eyes, but human relationships provide opportunities for even greater goodness than we can find by ourselves. It is obvious from this earliest story that God calls us to the greater goodness available in relationships with God and with other people.

This fact has a particular bearing on our approach to Bible study because it is very hard to get a clear, balanced view of God all by ourselves. Our minds and hearts are marvelous things, capable of great creativity and great distortion. But how many times have we thought something through in our own mind and become convinced of its unassailable brilliance, only to discover its flaws and foolishness when we tried to explain it to someone else? If that can happen in day-to-day thinking, consider its particular dangers in working with something as subject to misinterpretation as the Bible. We need a community around us when we approach the Lord through scripture.

There are, however, many ways to connect with that community. We cannot make the point that the Bible should be read routinely and then insist that it be done only in groups of six or more. There are clearly times when the Bible will—and even should—be read alone. The Daily Office in the Book of Common Prayer, for example, relies on a lectionary or list of Bible readings that can be read alone or in corporate worship. *Lectio divina* was designed for individual reading and has only recently been adapted to use in groups. Such private readings of scripture can satisfy the need for community in at least two ways.

The first is to be always aware of the community "in front of the text," the people who first spoke or wrote the words we read and the communities of people who first read or heard them. Whatever we might hear in our reading will have a connection to what they heard. In this regard a solitary reader with a decent commentary is able to be in touch with those original communities and the meanings that can enrich our own understandings. For daily reading I find that an annotated Bible provides just enough information to keep me from wandering too far afield.

In my personal reading of the Bible I use what I call the Post-it Note Technique. I read the Daily Office and look at each assigned passage as if it had a Post-it note saying "Frank—FYI—Jesus." That sets me to wondering why my Lord would want me to read this particular passage. Quite often, if the truth be told, I have no idea and guess that either Jesus got the wrong Frank or I have missed something he saw in it. For many years this was the case as I read the Psalms. I was especially put off by the psalmists' struggles with their enemies. Psalm 35 is one example among many. The writer asks God to fight those who are attacking him, claiming that they have spread a net for him and want him to fall into a pit. He sees malicious witnesses who charge him falsely, who mocked him gladly when he stumbled. The psalmist asks God to cut these enemies no slack, but to make their way dark and slippery while angels pursue them. I lead a fairly calm life, and while there are people I get along with better than others and there are those whose choices do not seem wise or good to me, I am not eager for their destruction. My enemies, if they could be called that, either lack the venom or have more social skills than those besetting the psalmist. I had trouble relating to the community "in front of the texts." This kind of struggle surely takes place in the world, but it seemed far from my world.

After long years of dutifully reading these passages that were just not connecting, I realized that my "enemies" of this kind were *inside* me rather than *around* me. The demons of my own temptations, impulses, weaknesses, ambitions, and self-promotion fit the text perfectly. They "do not speak peace" in my life, they "conceive deceitful words," they are the "roaring beasts" and "young lions" that circle my mind in the night. Struggling with the psalmist and his or her community allowed the Bible to speak once again with clarity and force. While it is true that a Bible study or sharing group could have pointed this out for me, I was not doing this reading in that context. I was alone but not without community. By myself I would have quit reading those psalms long ago. The people standing behind me in the mists of history, those who wrote the words and those who asked me to keep reading them, fulfilled an essential communal role as I studied the Bible without a group of contemporaries around me.

Secondly, it is widely known that those who read and ponder in isolation must be ready to share their insights with others before acting on them. A Cheyenne medicine man who had been at the Battle of the Little Big Horn was interviewed later in his life about the customs of his people. The results are in a wonderful little book called *Black Elk Speaks.* In it he describes the ritual of young men going out into the wilderness seeking a vision for their lives. The vision, no matter how dramatic or clear it might seem to the warrior, was not real or binding until it had been shared with the community and affirmed by them. It was a good rule for the Plains Indians and it is a good rule for the modern Bible reader.

Most of the time our individual reading of scripture will simply wash over us, refilling our souls with ancient freshness, reminding us of the basic dynamics of grace and faith, sin and salvation. But sometimes it points with startling clarity, a sense of urgent demand for action, for setting a new course; quite often, it is a dimly perceived but pressing message. In those cases, the solitary reader must call in the community for verification. Revelation is oftentimes like a suit we try on in the fluorescent lighting of the store, only to find that it does not look so good in the clear light of day. God, unlike the department store clerk, encourages us to take his Word outside before we buy it. The solitary reader of scripture wants a community in the wings so that messages can be tested.

Bible study today

While most of our attention will be devoted to identifiable methods and systems of studying the Bible, we must begin with our widest exposure to scripture, Sunday morning worship. For many Episcopalians, the only time they hear the biblical texts and have serious thought applied to them is during the Sunday Eucharist. In the Ministry of the Word (the first part of the service), all of the essential elements of good Bible study are present— but how well they are exercised from the lectern and pulpit or drawn upon from the pews is un-measurable, beyond the reminder that Thomas Bray's 1701 assessment of American Anglicans as "utterly destitute" of instruction in the Christian religion has ongoing support in many polls today. (I will leave it to you to reflect upon your own experience in this regard.)

There are, however, some developments that are making a difference throughout our church. In earlier times, worshippers brought their Bibles to church with them. Readings were introduced with the chapter and verse, thus giving the people in the pews a chance to read along with the lector and enhance their understanding by employing both auditory and visual senses. Many lay readers still solemnly give the full reference as if we were going to look them up, but the fact is that few of us carry Bibles to church on Sundays and most of us would be embarrassed at how long it would take to find the appointed lessons if we did. Most congregations use preprinted versions of the texts, a handy tool for use during both preparation for and participation in the service. In addition, sound systems are widely used even in the smallest of worship spaces, so that everyone should be able to hear. This is especially true if the reader remembers to read slowly and clearly.

In 2006 the General Convention of our church called for use of the *Revised Common Lectionary* (RCL) for our Sunday services. This arrangement of lessons literally puts us on the same page as most of our ecumenical brothers and sisters, and has the added advantage of enriching our readings. The RCL gives us an opportunity to follow some of the great stories of the Hebrew scriptures for several Sundays during the Season after Pentecost, thus opening a rich tradition that was otherwise denied those congregants who hear the Bible only on Sundays.

Preaching is the subject not only of a book in this series but of countless tomes, courses, articles, and after-church conversations. I have no intention of adding to that mix except to point out that like the Bible, a sermon is trying to reach the heart of the listener by going through the mind, an arduous journey to be sure. Most of the literature and commentary on preaching focuses on the speaker and there is much of value to be said in regard to what that one person does. However, during any sermon there are always more people in the pews than in the pulpit, which means that the sermon event involves more listening than speaking. A twelve-minute sermon delivered to a congregation of one hundred people involves twenty hours of listening (12 minutes times 100 people equals 1200 minutes, divided by 60 minutes/hour equals 20 hours).

Good preachers not only know how to speak, they also know how people hear. The point that has implications for our future relationship to scripture is that we must encourage parishioners to sharpen their listening skills.

Learning to be better hearers of the read word and the spoken word in the context of worship is important if we are to reach the full potential of our widest exposure to the Bible. Good sermon listening is critical listening. As the preacher has wrestled with the text, the listener should wrestle with the preacher. If you disagree with the preacher, figure out why and articulate what you think is true. If the sermon seems to be a jumble of unconnected dots, pick a dot and see if it has anything to tell you. The sermon that really has the power to convert is the one people preach to themselves after the homilist sits down. Learning to deliver this sermon-after-the-sermon is a skill that can help unleash the Bible's power in our church.

EDUCATION FOR MINISTRY

Education for Ministry, or EfM, as it is popularly known, is one of the most widely used and effective theological education programs outside the resident seminaries of the Episcopal Church. The course had its origins in the early 1970s, with early work based on the studies of Father Bernard Longeran SJ (1904–1984), who suggested that human knowledge comes from a combination of experience, understanding, and judgment. The Reverend Charles Winters led the development efforts that laid the foundation for EfM's emphasis on critical theological reflection rooted in small group study and prayer. The purpose from the beginning has been to provide quality theological education to empower the ministry of the baptized. The program is currently used in nine countries outside of the United States, where it has influenced over seventy thousand people. The full four-year course of study has been completed by over twenty thousand individuals, nearly one-third of the total. A professional staff at the University of the South and a network of scholar consultants maintain the high quality of its offerings.

A hallmark of the course, outside of its academic excellence, is the commitment required of its participants. Groups of six to twelve may meet regularly, or individuals may take advantage of an online connection. In either case the expectations are daunting. From two to five hours of study are needed for adequate preparation for the weekly sessions, which last about two hours. Sessions are devoted to group worship, discussion of the assigned content, and theological reflection. Each group has a mentor who must undergo at least eighteen hours of rigorous training before qualifying, followed by advanced training every eighteen months to remain certified.

In each thirty-six-week course there is an emphasis on exploring the biblical, doctrinal, and liturgical traditions of the church as they are expressed in the culture or context of the group taking the course. The position or convictions of the members of the group are honored and encouraged to deepen. A "parallel guide" for each session helps members to explore their personal connection to the texts. Sharing those insights with the group makes the experience more binding and the code of strict confidentiality makes in-depth sharing more likely.

The end result of the course is expected to be action: ministry in one form or another by the participants. In this regard EfM remains true to its origins as a method to prepare people for ministry, though it is now more widely used for lay ministry than ordained. A graduation certificate is presented to those who complete the work. In many congregations this is done in the context of corporate worship so that the connection between the work of the small EfM group and the life of the wider church is made clear.

Education for Ministry equips people for ministry and offers validation for those ministries through the sense of accomplishment as well as the certificate of graduation. It bears witness to the fact that the Bible must be approached in a serious way, taking traditional under-standings and biblical criticism into account. By the same token it connects scripture not only to our life in the world, but also to the church's ministry today.

EfM has been a successful instrument of study and basis for ministry for over thirty years. In spite of, or perhaps because of, its serious and heavy demands, thou-sands have enrolled, and an impressive percentage have completed its curriculum. As a Marine Corps recruiting slogan put it, "We don't take applications, only commit-ments." The timid and the tepid probably do not get very near an EfM group, and those who do think about dabbling in it are probably dissuaded by the fact that the substantial financial investment is to be paid up-front. It provides a place of informed refreshment for the well-educated who are willing and able to discipline their lives to undertake the equivalent of a college- or seminary-level course of study. It has a cerebral core that introduces its adherents to theological reflection techniques that can enrich their lives for as long as they breathe and believe. The Episcopal Church has long been deeply thankful for those who crafted this program, those who maintain its excellence, and especially for those who have drawn on its resources and blessed our church and world with the fruits of their work.

DISCIPLES OF CHRIST IN COMMUNITY (DOCC)

DOCC, as it is commonly known, was developed in 1974 by the Reverend John Jenkins of Trinity Episcopal Church in New Orleans, who was influenced by the charismatic renewal and Cursillo movements. Since then it has been used in over five hundred Episcopal congregations, touching the lives of as many as thirty thousand of us. It is a parish-based exploration of the biblical call to disciple-ship involving eighteen to twenty-four sessions, each with a thirty to forty-five minute presentation of content followed by an hour of small-group reflection and discussion.

Like its cousin, EfM, much of DOCC's material was developed at the University of the South. Similarities are apparent. Both require serious commitment on the part of leaders and participants. Small-group facilitators take eighteen hours of training. Those who think they might miss as many as two of the scheduled sessions are not encouraged to sign on. While outlines of the presentations are provided along with recorded lectures, it is assumed that the weekly presentations will be made by the clergy or trained lay theologians. The academic roots of both programs are represented in serious research and study, with a certificate of completion awarded after successful completion.

DOCC is a system designed to explore Christian discipleship in general and the discipleship of the participants in particular. It pays special attention to the biblical covenants and the theology of the kingdom of God expressed in the parables. The program gives equal emphasis to the centrality of community and the importance of individuality by encouraging what is called "active listening" in the small-group discussion. One of its means for connecting the ancient story and the modern world is to ask participants to craft parables Jesus might tell today. DOCC has a proven potential for transforming congregations through small-group Bible study. While doctrine has its place in the presentations, the major emphasis is on learning how to actively share the love of God rather than simply understanding dogma. Those who have responded to its offerings have felt the warmth of a mini-church where they have learned to articulate their faith, to agree and disagree in love, and to share in a caring, serving community. More than one parish has found that the community and communication lessons learned in DOCC have paid enormous dividends in times of congregational stress and anxiety.

One of the key reasons for DOCC's success lies in the defined roles of clergy and laity. The small groups are lay-led and the presentations are clergy-led. Keeping the clergy out of the group discussions, while turning them over to trained laity, is a brilliant move. While exceptions abound, clergy can unintentionally dominate faith-sharing groups by the weight ordination has acquired over the past several centuries. There is a tendency to think that the clergy know the right answers or have a pipeline to God installed at seminary. This mystique, ill-founded though it may be, can be hard on small faith-sharing groups. DOCC has found a way to address this issue and for that we may be thankful.

Like EfM, its structural requirements keep it from being broadly available. The level of commitment required keeps it from being any kind of a resource for seekers. And, in spite of the training required, not every person who might volunteer possesses the skills required for leading a small group. Its track record, however, provides convincing evidence that the results of a parish commitment to DOCC are well worth the effort required.

BIBLE WORKBENCH

In 1979 a group of Christian educators met in North Carolina to discuss the development of a new and dynamic approach to Bible study. All had experience in The Educational Center in St. Louis and were influenced by the Reverend Charles Penniman, its director in the 1950s, whose idea that "the student is the curriculum" became almost a mantra for the designers. Penniman's theory honors the unique nature of each Bible study group and of each person in the group. The result is an approach to Bible study that makes no attempt to reach consensus or to impose an interpretation on participants. Each person is encouraged to engage scripture in his or her own way. In this regard Bible Workbench is an excellent example of a method as opposed to a system. The program is now a centerpiece of The Educational Center's offerings.

The approach itself is not that unique. Participants are taken through three questions:

* What is going on in the text?

* How is that taking place in the world today?

* How is that happening in my life today?

This pattern is replicated in many study programs as a way of bridging the gap between the community "in front of the text" and our own world. It includes the key element of expectant reading in that it assumes that what went on in the text is in fact going on in our lives, and it relies on fulfilling that expectation through responses to leading questions. What is unique in Bible Workbench is its intentional focus on preachers and its inclusion of current resources it calls "parallel reading."

Subscribers are mailed packets that include materials focused on one lesson in the Sunday *Revised Common Lectionary.* Scholarly background material on the text as well as questions for group leaders or individual readers are provided. These questions are so complete, the designers suggest that leadership in a group rotate among members, indicating that anyone can follow their directions. The parallel readings include passages from books, poetry, and current articles that shed light on the text. To my knowledge, no other program widely used in the Episcopal Church offers a combination of current biblical scholarship and contemporary quotable resources. Few preachers would fail to benefit from such a weekly prompting, and few Bible study groups would not be enriched by the thoughts of modern writers and poets.

Subscriptions to Bible Workbench may be annual, semiannual, or for a church season. While the main emphasis is on adults, a Teen Text for high school students and a Kid's Text for younger children are also available. Since each week's discussion is based on a discrete text, consistent attendance is not required. Nor is a biblical background necessary, because of the scholarly material included. It should be noted that the scholars, including Marcus Borg, Walter Brueggemann, John Dominic Crossan, Elaine Pagels, and Walter Wink, are widely known but properly identified with less traditional/more innovative interpretations of scripture.

Penniman's emphasis on honoring individual learning is represented in some groups by placing a candle in the center of the gathering. Members are encouraged to speak to the candle rather than each other as a way of engaging the text without getting sidetracked or argumentative. The lack of interpersonal exchange is another reason untrained members can all take turns at leading. Participants are encouraged to speak as openly as they can, which allows an experience of deep bonding even though personal interactions are limited.

The homiletic principle suggested is described as simply "delivering" a text rather than interpreting it. Preachers are encouraged to develop sermons on the model of the Bible Workbench material, which means providing the congregation with questions rather than answers, assuming that each congregant will make the essential connections to his or her own life. This is Penniman's "the student is the curriculum" carried into the Ministry of the Word in liturgy. I doubt that all preachers would align themselves completely with this philosophy, if only because of the different motivations of people in Bible study groups and people in worship.

Nevertheless, the point is worth including in a preacher's bag of options.

Bible Workbench has a lamentably small subscriber base. One reason is that its use of current articles requires copyright permissions. This makes an internet program prohibitive because copyright costs increase substantially when granted for the broad access the web allows. The program deserves a wider role in the life of our church for its excellence and for its innovative approach to connecting the ancient and modern worlds.

LECTIO DIVINA

The words *lectio divina* mean "holy reading," and they come to us through the Rule of Saint Benedict, a sixth-century document for monastics which has had enormous influence in the life of the church well beyond the cloister. Studies, interpretations, and adaptations of the Benedictine Rule have become increasingly popular in the Episcopal Church in recent years and have helped *lectio divina* to be a significant resource for us. While originally designed for use by individuals who were living in religious communities, it can be adapted for the kind of prayer and scripture groups we find in modern congregations.

Benedict's approach must be understood first of all as a discipline of prayer. Indeed, most refer to *lectio divina* as a way of praying the scriptures rather than a way of studying them. In that context the first step is *lectio,* literally "reading." But this is not simply reading to ingest information. It means listening with the "ear of the heart," which requires silence—both internal and external. Adherents also make a distinction between hearing and listening. One hears a playbill but listens to a concert. The latter requires more effort, the kind of effort expected in holy reading. If the discipline of centering prayer comes to your mind, you would not be too far off.

The second step is called *meditatio,* or meditation. This involves letting a word or phrase in the text rise in your consciousness and pondering it in your heart, as Mary did. Those of us with a less mystical bent would call it thinking, but we would be wrong if we supposed meditation meant analysis or problem solving. It is more like wondering, more like the way our minds wonder—and wander into reflection—as we listen to a symphony or gaze at a sunset.

The third step is *oratio,* prayer, in which the reader makes an offering out of the experience and lays it before God. At this point the deeper we reach into ourselves for that offering the better.

The final period is *contemplatio,* or contemplation. In this context it means to rest in God, to simply be glad to be held in God's love. It is to enjoy the privilege cited in Psalm 131:3, "I still my soul and make it quiet, like a child upon its mother's breast; my soul is quieted within me" (BCP 785).

As we turn to Scripture in expectancy of a living encounter with God, we will begin to wonder if God meets us in the same empowering and transforming way in other settings as well. Might we trust that it is God's desire to be active and present, speaking to each of us in a personal and potentially transforming way in our daily life? — *Norvene Vest*

These steps are not rigid and are often adapted by choice or blurred by the Spirit. They were first articulated in the twelfth century as a guide to Benedict's admonitions, rather like dance steps in a book that precede actual dancing.

As you can see, this method is not designed for the man or woman on the go. These are not what a friend of mine calls "popcorn prayers" that are randomly tossed heavenward. Benedict and those who have lived his rule over the centuries give high value to the patient expectation *lectio divina* requires. Devotees are aware of a gentle oscillation back and forth between spiritual activity (meditation and prayer) and spiritual receptivity (reading and contemplation). Many of us would say that we do not have time for such a discipline, and that might be true. It is, however, more honest if we speak in terms of priorities rather than time itself. We may choose to give priority to other activities, and some of them may be quite compelling—raising children, making a living, boldly exploring new worlds. I do not suggest that everyone should set aside every day the kind of time *lectio divina* requires, but I am suggesting that many if not most of us could find more time for this way of reading if we reordered our priorities.

The most unique feature of Benedict's discipline is in its reversal of the concept of relevance. The presenting question for most Bible studies and for most of us who turn to the Bible is, "What does it say about my life?" We want to know how the Bible fits into our world, how it speaks to our issues and needs. Praying the Bible provides a completely different context. The question becomes, "How does my life fit into the Bible?" The focus is not on my mind but on the mind of Christ, not on my heart but on the heart of God. The belief is that when we are attuned to the will and the ways of God, to the ongoing life of creation, we will be healthier, more whole, and closer to what we were created to be. It takes almost literally the conclusion of William James in *Varieties of Religious Experience* that "there is something wrong with us as we naturally stand" and that "we are saved from that wrongness by making proper connection with the higher powers." The question is not how the Bible message fits in our life, but how we fit into the Bible message. Such an approach has obvious merit, but it does not "pay off" in the short term. Time is required for the discipline and patience is required for the benefit. I doubt that it is necessary to point out, but unrewarding methods do not stay with us for fifteen hundred years. This method has an impressive track record.

As I mentioned above, *lectio divina* was designed for individuals who were living in community. They were surrounded by people who understood Benedict's method and the nasty bogs one can get into on a spiritual journey. Few of us have that resource so close at hand. This is an important point because *lectio divina* is pure method. It does not provide any guidance about what one might discover while listening or pondering. And there is precious little in the Rule itself that would help us to sort out healthy and unhealthy offerings. Few of us can keep the image of God as Father from being colored by our experiences with our biological fathers. The same is true of the great healing stories and our own unhealed maladies. *Lectio divina* is a powerful way to encounter God in scripture. Because of this its adherents should have some anchor to windward—a spiritual director, a soul friend, or a praying community—who can help to provide illumination for the darker corners of our spiritual journey.

THE ALPHA COURSE

"Phenomenon" is probably a better description of Alpha than "course" or "curriculum." In 1990 a young Anglican clergyman named Nicky Gumbel took over a long-standing ministry at Holy Trinity Church, Brompton in London. The original course was designed for new Christians, but in Gumbel's skilled hands it became a course for those outside the church. His prolific teachings and writings have turned it into a major faith-and-culture factor around the world. Over 11 million people in 163 countries have participated in its winning combination of casual format and carefully scripted witness. Holy Trinity parish has been rewarded with a widely recognized acronym (HTB), and the course has been adapted for use in the workplace, prisons, the military, and on college campuses.

In our terms, it is a system disguised as a method. The target group is the seeker, or even beyond that, the mildly curious. Anyone who has ever wondered if there is more to life than what they now know is a likely candidate. Participants are encouraged to ask any question that occurs to them. The opening presentation takes up the issue of Christianity as boring or irrelevant. This wide-open approach is one of the several points of genius in the program. The agenda of the designers is made clear, however, in the boast that 50 percent of those who take the course make a commitment to Jesus as Lord. In this it is a system committed to conversion.

A major emphasis in Alpha and a major reason for its success is the practice of hospitality. This often ignored aspect of faith and evangelism is the first expression of the program and the first experience of those who attend. The format is casual and welcoming. Church hierarchy, trappings, and, to a considerable extent, doctrine are not in evidence. There are no fees. Gatherings begin with an unhurried hour-long meal followed by a forty-five minute presentation and then another hour of small-group discussion. Details of the presentations are given in the leader's guide, and videos by Nicky Gumbel himself are also available. The term for such an approach is "permission evangelism," which means that participants join and remain of their own free will without any real or implied pressure. Warm and genuine hospitality make permission evangelism possible.

Another significant aspect of the course is its acceptance of the fact that most people do not have any real knowledge or even a positive impression of Christianity. While our buildings may be on practically every corner, we have minority status in the thinking of the world. The starting point, therefore, is very basic. As in Saint Paul's fledgling community in Corinth, the spiritual diet is milk, not solid food (1 Corinthians 3:2). While the course is pointedly nondenominational, it is decidedly evangelical and charismatic. Alpha's reach is more wide than deep. Its substance is given clarity by avoiding nuance and offering a straight path between right and wrong. It is on this point that Alpha's major critics take their stand. There is more than a hint of biblical literalism in its teaching. Complicated doctrines like the atonement are given a single interpretation ("substitutionary"), when in fact Christianity includes a variety of understandings. While Alpha's views are legitimate parts of the life of the church, it is not quite fair to imply, as Alpha does, that they represent "the" Christian view.

On the other hand, one must remember Alpha's central goal which is to reach the unchurched, a goal it has had remarkable success in attaining. The seeker and the mildly curious are not likely to be drawn to the debates of faith but to its affirmations. To their credit, the designers of Alpha encourage follow-up sessions that can iron out or clarify some of the softer issues of understanding.

While the scriptures are quoted and referred to throughout the course, there is only one evening session of the basic course which considers the Bible directly. "Why and how should I read the Bible?" begins with classic Alpha nonthreatening discussion starters, asking participants about their experiences with the Bible. "Have you ever read it? Is it more rule book or love letter?" The Parable of the Sower (Mark 4:1–8, 13–20) is used for reflection on various responses to the Word.

Alpha takes up a central theme of this book when it considers how one might hear God speak through the Bible. Regular, expectant reading in a special solitary place, with some commentaries at hand, is the framework. Questions not unlike other popular study programs are applied: "What does it say? What does it mean? How does it apply?" Participants are then encouraged to act on what they have concluded. Alpha's techniques in this regard are solid, tested, and proven in a variety of disciplines. Its theological suppositions, however, are less representative, which has encouraged some congregations to adopt the Alpha technique while filling in different theologies. It is a tribute to the genius of Alpha's approach that this can be done.

Alpha has carved out a niche on the borders between Christ and culture, the sacred and the secular, belief and unbelief. It has proven itself an effective agent for real growth for those who find themselves on those borders. Those whose faith is a little more clearly established may question its depth, and those with a different theological view may question its breadth, but few can deny that Alpha is making a difference in our church and in the world.

COMMENTARIES AND STUDY BIBLES

The seventh chapter of Mark's gospel begins with a story of Pharisees who were horrified that Jesus' disciples ate without washing their hands. The third verse is a peculiar addition, most likely inserted by a scribe making a copy of the original text. Concerned that his Gentile readers would not understand the Pharisees' reaction, he provides the following:

> For the Pharisees, and all the Jews, do not eat unless they thoroughly wash their hands, thus observing the tradition of the elders; and they do not eat anything from the market unless they wash it; and there are also many other traditions that they observe, the washing of cups, pots, and bronze kettles. (Mark 7:3–4)

This illuminating insertion is a part of a great tradition of Bible commentary. Jewish scholars had long been adding interpretive comments to the Hebrew scriptures, and the New Testament writers followed in their footsteps.

Christian scholars have generated a multitude of commentaries in the ensuing generations, and few modern readers dare to stray very far from them, lest the gap between the world of the text and the world of the reader become too great. The number of commentaries available today is staggering, and listing them would be well beyond the scope of this book. Commentaries come in all shapes and sizes, and follow a wide variety of formats, from academic studies to devotional reflection. When specific reflections by a writer or questions designed to deepen reflections by the reader are added to the scriptures, the result is a Bible (or certain texts of the Bible) designed for study, usually called a study Bible. Their numbers are also great and a full review is not possible here, but I would like to draw your attention to some types that are in current use in the Episcopal Church.

One of the most widely used biblical study/reflection resources in our church is the booklet *Forward Day by Day*. Published by Forward Movement Publications, it has over twenty thousand individual subscribers and many more who take advantage of its offerings through church tract racks. The quarterly issues in both English and Spanish provide meditations on daily readings, usually taken from the Daily Office lectionary in the Book of Common Prayer. Its particular advantage is its brevity (not more than 250 words per meditation) and compact size, which make it usable in a busy day and portable in a mobile life. Because each volume has a different author, the booklets are seldom stale, though they are uneven in depth of insight. Forward Movement also has a variety of pamphlets on the Bible, and their "Books of the Bible" series provides brief introductions to the key books of both the Old and New Testament.

The *Serendipity Bible,* published by Serendipity House, uses the respected New International Version, which has, broadly speaking, an evangelical base. This Bible includes over thirty thousand questions for small-group discussion, as well as scholarly commentaries throughout the text. Readers are asked to enter into the feeling level of the stories in order to encounter God personally. The index includes structured courses for certain readers (men, women, singles), circumstances (workplace, marriage), issues (church life, coping), biblical figures (David, Paul, prophets), and theologies (Trinity, atonement). The *Serendipity Bible* has been around since 1973 and has a valuable contribution to make as the focal point or a resource for group or individual study.

Zondervan's *The Student Bible* has a similar evangelical base and is specifically geared to college students, but has value for older seekers as well. The commentary, introductions to each book, short essays, and discussion questions were written by Philip Yancey and Tim Stafford, editor and senior writer for *Christianity Today.* As with *Serendipity,* the text is the New International Version. In addition to study of specific texts, there are three reading plans suggested, lasting six weeks, six months, or three years. A subject guide or topical concordance is included for those who want to pursue a more independent study.

The *Focus Bible Study Series,* published by Morehouse Publishing, follows a workbook format that provides a summary of each section with questions for consideration. Journal meditations are included, which are pages for one's own reflections based on thoughtful questions ("In what ways are you a witness to Jesus' resurrection?"). The opening line to a prayer is given, with the intent that one's own prayer would follow ("Lord, teach me to pray like Jesus, that I might be filled with your Holy Spirit and empowered for your service"). The format and the specific reflection tools are unusual among study Bibles.

The *Kids' Study Bible,* published by Zondervan, makes use of what is called a transliteration, which means a paraphrase of the New International Version, in order to provide simpler language for young readers. It is also useful for semiliterate adults and those learning English as a second language. The art and questions, called Brain Game Sections, are clearly for the young and would have to be adapted for adult readers. Even with a young audience in mind, the designers have not flinched at the difficult passages. The Brain Game after the story of David and Bathsheba asks what God might have thought about David's behavior.

The commentaries of William Barclay, published by Westminster Press, provide the reflections of the author in narrative form. First published in his native Scotland in 1978, Barclay's combination of his own translation of the text, commentary, and reflection have made these volumes a classic.

The volumes of the ... *For Everyone* series, published by SPCK Publishing in London, were written by N.T. Wright, Anglican Bishop of Durham and prolific author and lecturer. These books are a more current expression of the genre developed by William Barclay. Written for a person "who wouldn't normally read a book with footnotes and Greek words in it," this series is an easy and thoughtful read. There is one volume for each book of the New Testament, and one can only assume that the Hebrew scriptures will not be far behind. Bishop Wright is a scholar of the first rank, often paired with his good friend and theological opposite, Marcus Borg, in debates and point-counterpoint essays, with the bishop taking the more traditional view. His insights seldom fail to inform and deepen even the most serious student of scripture.

This very brief look at study Bibles reveals a peculiar pattern: the field is dominated by those who have a more traditional approach to scripture and its interpretation.

There is certainly nothing wrong with traditional views, but where are the innovators, the liberals whose fresh insights have so challenged and enriched our church? The Jesus Seminar has written much, but little of it is intended for the same audience as the study and reflection Bibles. Are new ideas too fresh for common consumption, or too complex and nuanced for the straight question-and-answer style of this field? Or is it a genre that no one with liberal viewpoints has taken seriously enough to prepare? Study Bibles are a major resource in the life of our church. Hopefully they will someday include the full range of biblical interpretation in our church.

AFRICAN BIBLE STUDY

During World War I, France was the epicenter of carnage and chaos at a level the world had never seen before and has seldom seen since. It is all the more remarkable that during such a time a Frenchman wrote a prayer beginning with lines that would become famous: "Lord, make me an instrument of your peace...." The individual's name, if it was ever widely known, is now forgotten. The extraordinary generosity and vulnerability of the prayer, however, reminded people of Francis of Assisi, so the prayer was attributed to him. In the strange way of the world, that designation is a compliment to both the real writer of the prayer and to Saint Francis. The African Bible study method has a similar mythic background. Common lore says that it was introduced at a Lambeth Conference by African bishops. Some say that it originated with Native Americans. In either case, it is a compliment to both groups because the method is refreshing, rewarding, and powerful.

The roots of what has come to be known as the African Bible study method are many, including the liberation theology of the late 1960s and beyond, which influenced so much of current approaches to scripture, although the

African Bible study has none of the economic focus of liberation theology. It is also indebted to what is called inductive Bible study, which begins with one's life and moves toward God's revelation rather than the more academic other way around. Contextual theology, which treats life experience as having authority equal to that of the biblical text, has played a part in it as well. It is worth noting that many contextual theologians are based in South Africa. The Lambeth Conference of 1988 did introduce small-group Bible study to its agenda for the world's Anglican bishops. This group format was a sharp departure from the lectures that had served as Bible study in prior conferences, and had the reflective, sharing aspect that characterizes the African method. It was, however, developed by a design team made up of bishops from throughout the Anglican Communion rather than an all-African contingent. While its roots are in many cultures, most people think of this method as African, a tribute to the respect with which the world regards the power of scripture in that part of the Body of Christ.

The method itself is simple and direct. A passage is read aloud slowly. Each person identifies a word or phrase that stands out for them and shares it with the group. There is no discussion, just sharing. The passage is read aloud again, hopefully from a different translation and by a different voice. People now share something of the manner in which the word or phrase relates to their life. Again there is no discussion, just sharing. After a third reading, participants reflect on what God might be calling them to do through this passage. The session ends with prayer for one another and a concluding group prayer or blessing.

The genius of the African Bible study method is the emphasis on sharing and listening rather than discussion. There is no way to be wrong in such a group. The one who speaks is the only expert in the room about what the passage may be saying to him or her. In addition, listening creates a powerful bond among people. The African Bible study method assumes the active presence of the Holy Spirit in the encounter with scripture. It is an assumption that is seldom disappointed, especially when the human desire to debate is taken out of the picture. It is a method as opposed to a system because it makes no assumptions as to outcome. The simplicity, faith, and openness of this method make it a most attractive and effective instrument of faith in the church.

It does not, however, stand alone for long. What is missing is the kind of intellectual engagement of the text and the community "in front of the text" that keeps us from trying to balance our faith on the narrow beam of our own thoughts and experiences. Hopefully, the fresh sense of engagement with the Word will lead people to want to study that Word, to know it better, to be able to reach more deeply into it. The African Bible study method itself does not require or suggest such a step, but the process is dangerous without it. One part of the wisdom of this approach is that it puts the reward of reading the Bible up front. Everybody is encouraged to hear something, and hearing something while reading the Bible is the source of its ancient claim upon us. It is much easier to get people who have been touched by scripture to study it than it is to get people who study scripture to be touched by it. The African Bible study method has one of the right formulas, as long as the study takes place at some point.

GOSPEL BASED DISCIPLESHIP

Gospel Based Discipleship is the African Bible study method passed through the cultural filter of indigenous people. Developed by National Church staff member John Robertson, Bishop Mark McDonald, and several others, it is the kind of application that must gladden the heart of a church seeking to affirm its multicultural identity. Gospel Based Discipleship's most significant expansion of the African Bible study method is setting it in a liturgical context. The material, provided by the Native Ministries Office, includes *A Disciple's Prayer Book,* which follows very closely the Daily Devotions for Individuals and Families in the Book of Common Prayer (pages 136–140) but includes prayers drawn from indigenous traditions. In addition to the book, a *Gathering Prayer Bookmark* provides a highly portable and usable format.

While insisting that it is neither a program nor a Bible study but "an encounter with the Gospel," it proves to be a Bible study program that makes that encounter more likely, more real, and more powerful. Although set in the context of liturgy and the larger context of the church year, the steps are essentially those of the African Bible study method. The lectionary-assigned text is read and people are asked to share the words or ideas that they heard most clearly. It is read again and the question becomes more pointed. "What is Jesus (or the Gospel) saying to you?" After a third reading, people are asked to reveal what Jesus or the gospel is calling them to do. As with the African Bible study method, the emphasis is on listening to others and sharing one's own response. It is not about debate. Reading in different translations is encouraged, with a specific recommendation that *The Message* (NavPress's energetic paraphrase of scripture by the Presbyterian pastor, scholar, and author Eugene Peterson) be used for one of the readings. I would hope that the paraphrase would not be read until after more broad-based translations have been heard. Such loose paraphrases are good for enlivening a passage and bringing it home in a powerful way, but they are not well-suited for focusing on a specific word or phrase, as the first question in Gospel Based Discipleship asks people to do.

Gospel Based Discipleship is, in fact, more than a Bible study. It is used in ordination discernment processes and as a spiritual discipline for individuals, groups, congregations, and dioceses. Its lineage as a child of the African Bible study method and grandchild of liberation theology does not obscure its specific contributions of a liturgical setting and a rich draw on indigenous traditions. If you liked the African Bible study method, you will love Gospel Based Discipleship.

IGNATIAN SPIRITUALITY

Ignatius was born to a noble family in the Spanish city of Loyola in 1491, the year before Columbus set sail on his first voyage of discovery. The young man grew up with the excesses that the New World made possible in Spain. At the age of twenty-five he was seriously wounded in a battle with the French. With little to do in his convalescence but read and little to read but religious works, the young soldier found himself drawn to a deep commitment to Jesus Christ. He applied his military training to his religious vocation and developed a rigorous spiritual discipline that is at the heart of the Society of Jesus, which he founded, and that has greatly influenced many non-Jesuits who make use of his insights.

In 1522 he began recording his *Spiritual Exercises.* I say "recording" because Ignatius felt they were more the result of revelation than an intellectual effort on his part. These exercises include, as the name implies, much more than Bible study, but they have a profound point to make for any student of the Bible. The exercises are applicable to every method one might use to examine one's conscience, including the reading of scripture. They are the centerpiece of the thirty-day retreat that is the *haj* or trip to Mecca for every follower of Ignatius's path.

The specific gift of Ignatian spirituality to Bible study in the Episcopal Church and beyond is the creative use of imagination as a way of entering into the biblical narrative. The Reverend Margot Critchfield describes the Ignatian experience with scripture in this way:

> The idea of entering into scripture imaginatively is by no means unique to Ignatius, but what he did with it was revolutionary. In his *30-Day Spiritual Exercises,* Ignatius developed a highly effective method for the making of disciples, the transforming of souls, the conversion of ordinary people that employs this method of imaginative contemplation—affective knowing—in a unique and systematic way. Beginning with the annunciation and incarnation, one is invited to *experience with Jesus* his birth, his life, his death, and his resurrection—all with astonishing detail, lucidity, and power. The result of this *affective experience* of Jesus is nothing short of a conversion experience—a passionate desire to seek and do his will in all things.[8]

As with many approaches to scripture, Ignatius assumed that the Holy Spirit was present in the study. His particular insight was that imagination can consistently be flint to the Spirit's steel and that sparks would fly. Five hundred years of field testing provide ample proof of his idea.

It is important to remember that Ignatius's use of imagination as a way of entering into the life of Christ is set in the context of a wider spiritual discipline. While it is possible to adapt the standard thirty-day retreat to a daily routine in a busy life, the use of imagination is always in context. Ignatius employed imagination in a unique way but he did not copyright it. Anyone can employ the technique as a way of meeting the Lord. Biblical events outside of the gospels may profitably be entered through the portal of imagination. It is not, however, a toy to be confused with daydreaming, fantasy, or the kind of one-act dramas that often take shape in our minds. Ignatius and his followers have shown us the power of this method. Because of its power it belongs in the larger context of spiritual discipline.

BIBLE STUDY WITH CHILDREN

I will be considering *Catechesis of the Good Shepherd* and *Godly Play* in a single section because they have so much in common and it will be easier to compare and contrast these two excellent children's programs. The beginning was in Italy in 1954 when Sofia Cavalletti, a Hebrew scholar, and Gianna Gobbi, a disciple of children's educator Maria Montessori, began to collaborate in the field of religious education for children. The Montessori theory of honoring the person and potential of a child was expanded to include a capacity for spirituality. Rather than treating the child as an empty vessel to be filled with adult lore, the natural instinct for God that is in each child was affirmed and encouraged. Dr. Cavalletti's serious academic background assured that the classroom did not become another "Lord of the Flies" in which children were free to run amok. Children are guided to parables, narratives, and liturgical practices that are well-grounded and age-appropriate. Dr. Jerome Berryman, an Episcopal priest, studied under Dr. Cavalletti in 1971–72 and developed *Godly Play* as an experiment with and extension of her work.

A key to the success of both programs is the setting, referred to as the "atrium" in *Catechesis of the Good Shepherd* because that is the place in early house churches where instruction was offered. Everything in the space is child-size with an educational role. Manipulatives, or objects the child can personally handle, are important— figures representing biblical characters, small communion vessels, sheep folds, tents, scrolls, maps, and so on. The room is so central to the program that multi-use is discouraged, so that it remains a child's sacred space. Many *Catechesis* programs are part of a school or after-school curricula where it is offered daily. In a congregation that focuses on Sunday activities, the designation of space may raise stewardship of buildings issues. The use of space for a brief period once a week must be considered against the cost of that space and the congregation's priorities. It is a significant affirmation of these programs that many churches make that commitment.

The format in both programs roughly follows the outline of the liturgy: gathering, presentation of the lesson, response, prayer, and departure. *Godly Play* emphasizes what is called the "feast" (which is a snack), but *Catechesis* does not. The tie in to what children experience in worship is important for reinforcement of the teaching as well as deepening their worship experience.

The role of adults is to support the child's process of discovery rather than "teach" in the traditional classroom sense. This requires significant training of the adult leaders and constitutes one of the major differences between the two programs. *Catechesis* has no teacher's manual. Classroom leaders are expected to prepare their own course material, from lesson plans to manipulatives. Certification for such a role requires about one hundred hours of training. *Godly Play* provides teacher resources and requires eighteen hours of instruction. One could reasonably wonder about working four times as long to get basically the same result. The answer is that the extra training is worth it. As Dorothy Linthicum wrote in *Episcopal Teacher,* trainees "find that their own spirituality is challenged and deepened. Their knowledge of the church and the Bible is expanded. Their relationships with children and youth and each other grow as they intensify their connection with God."[9] The authors of *Catechesis* wrote that after thirty-five years in the program they still learn from children and have the opportunity to "sense the presence of a force, mysterious and silent, which does not belong to us...the inestimable privilege [of] beholding the presence of God."[10] I am not in a position to say that *Catechesis* training is four times as rewarding as *Godly Play* training. Devotees of one would say it is, fans of the other would say it is not. It is worth noting that *Catechesis* is being used in thirty-two countries and in multiple denominations. *Godly Play* is younger but already in over a dozen countries and is used by several denominations. With such a great cloud of witnesses, there can be little doubt that the training and the programs are worth it.

LESSON PLANS FOR SMALL CONGREGATIONS

The Episcopal Church has not officially produced Christian education materials since the late 1960s, when the decision was made to rely on various educational and publishing resources in the church rather than the central office. As this chapter attests, the decision has not deprived us of worthwhile material for education in general and Bible study in particular. There is, however, a lectionary-based curriculum that, while developed especially for small congregations, has much to offer churches as well as schools, camps, and conferences. The program was developed by ECCE (Episcopal Council for Christian Education) and the Ministries with Young People Cluster of the Episcopal Church. The former is made up of representatives appointed by the presidents of each of the nine provinces of the Episcopal Church; the latter are staff members at the Episcopal Church Center in New York. The result is a traditional and solidly structured program that makes creativity on the part of leaders neither necessary nor precluded.

The program is congregation-based, with a much wider reach than the more disciplined congregational programs like DOCC. Lesson Plans for Small

Congregations is for any Sunday in any congregation. Unlike DOCC it adapts to the fact that people do not come to church or stay for education every Sunday. Each class presentation stands on its own. Each session contains a lesson plan with questions and activities for younger children, older children, and adults. It is a system rather than a method because it knows the right answers to even the discussion questions, and includes them in the leader's guide. In the case of children's lessons, brief but helpful background information on age-appropriate educational and spiritual development is provided. Learning goals are not well spelled out, so the novice leader may not always know where the group is headed or why it is going there.

One great and unique advantage of this program is that classes for adults and young people consider the same text on any given Sunday. This facilitates the enormously important step of family discussions at home. One measure of the significance of family discussion in the spiritual and theological formation of children can be seen in a simple running of the numbers. If a child were to spend two hours at church every week from birth to age eighteen, never missing a Sunday or cutting so much as a minute from the full exposure to worship and education, he or she will be in church a total of 2,172 hours. During that same time period, if they are like most people in our culture, they will watch well over twenty thousand hours of television. With odds like that, it is difficult to see how the church can be the determining influence in a child's moral and spiritual formation unless there is active support at home. This Episcopal Church curriculum helps to make that vital connecting step, and for that alone it deserves our attention.

The several Bible study approaches discussed here can be considered as concentric circles. Alpha is the outer circle, with its emphasis on hospitality for the seeker. Ministry of the Word in liturgy, Bible Workbench, study Bibles, and the Lesson Plans for Small Congregations are in the next circle, providing sustenance in the context of routine congregational life. Inside of that circle we can place the Ignatian use of imagination, African Bible Study, and Gospel Based Discipleship as parishioners expose them-selves to the transforming power of scripture. *Lectio divina,* Education for Ministry, and DOCC make up the inner circle, where the deeply committed can wrap the Bible around their lives by wrapping their lives around the Bible.

This is no more than a device for thinking about the several disciplines in prominent use in the Episcopal Church today. Exceptions to my categories abound. Surely DOCC has touched seekers and Alpha has been the stage for profound encounters with the Lord. I suggest this set of concentric circles as a way of preparing for the next chapter, which is about how our church might approach the Bible and Bible study in the coming century.

Rethinking Our Attitudes

"This changes everything except the way people think" is said to have been Albert Einstein's cogent observation after the dropping of the atomic bomb on Japan at the end of World War II. The internal realities about how the universe functions and holds together achieved a startling new dimension, while the external realities about what was possible had been expanded beyond imagination. The only thing that had not changed was the way people thought about the universe and its potential.

On an entirely different scale, the same can be said about the Bible and the Episcopal Church. In chapter two we looked at the principles that have guided our tradition for the past five hundred years. In chapter three we reviewed some of the methods and systems in current use and how they apply those principles. The two together give us a picture of where we are now, and the picture they give is one of rich resources and various proven approaches. We do not need new principles nor do we need a whole new set of programs. But in order for the Bible to play a new, dynamic, and transformative role in the future of our church, some changes need to take place. What are the essential attitudes and tools for transforming our approach to scripture in order that scripture transforms our approach to life?

The first changes, as Einstein suggested, must be in our thinking, in our understanding of the principles that have guided us thus far. What we have received from our spiritual ancestors is solid, but this new century has placed demands upon that inheritance and provided enrichments to it that our forebears did not know. Each of the principles must be extended and then applied to the programs we use if we are to meet the challenges and opportunities of the twenty-first century. These extensions are the tools that will hone our methods and systems for future use. In this chapter I will examine some of those changes and the kind of new thinking we need to apply to the various approaches to Bible study.

Because of the rapidity of change over a very short time, the twenty-first century is a very different time from those that have preceded it. Some of those differences are obvious and have been developed in earlier chapters. We know that we are far from the community "in front of the text," for example. They lived in what they thought was a one-world universe, with all of creation revolving around the earth, which they assumed to be flat like a plate rather than round like a ball. Galileo's development of the telescope in the sixteenth century and Leeuwenhoek's work with the microscope in the seventeenth revealed a world inconceivable to our ancestors, with human life suspended somewhere between microbes and the Milky Way.

Further, our forebears believed that everything of significance and many things of insignificance happened because God specifically decreed them. They did not have the same sense of the workings of nature and of "natural causes" that we do today, so for them the logical response to drought, disease, or defeat was to appeal to the God who they believed had caused them—generally in anger. We are far less clear about the role God plays in the ups and downs of life today because we suspect that there are far more possibilities than divine pleasure/displeasure to explain them.

We see these differences of understanding in the historical accounts as well. The chroniclers of the Hebrew Bible, for example, present the history of the kings of Israel and Judah as primarily a record of faithfulness versus apostasy, rather than an "objective" recounting of events. Likewise, the social norms of their culture were quite different from our own. Saint Paul seems to think he is being quite subtle in his appeal to Philemon on behalf of his runaway slave Onesimus, while to our ears it seems more than a little heavy-handed. Another difference is that our thinking has been strongly influenced by the discoveries of Charles Darwin, who interpreted the direction of life as one of evolution into an unknown future. Our ancestors understood life's direction as a pilgrim's progress of return to an edenic state we once occupied and, by God's grace, will occupy again. Add to these the multiple layers of biblical translations mixed with the Sahara-like shifting of the meaning of words within a language, the elusive trail back to the original documents, and the basic inadequacy of any words to convey the deepest matters of the mind and heart, and we have some glimpse of the realities that make Bible reading a challenge.

Yet, the Bible remains the Word, the meeting ground, where God still speaks so that the most modern and even postmodern ears can hear. The various methods and systems we have for reading the Bible are proof-positive that the thicket of differences grown up between us and the community "in front of the text" can be breached. The countless numbers who have found solace, direction, insight, and correction in its pages do not need to be told that the Bible can still be a living, dynamic reality. While some among us may have trivialized the role of scripture in our day by reducing it to a plodding formality of corporate worship, a reference book for understanding English literature, or the background of favorite hymns, God has not. God still salts its words with messages and meanings, uses its images to illumine both the ordinary and the extraordinary, lets its cadences empower the rhythms of life, and whispers with a still, small voice in mysteries.

The gulf that lies between the ancient text and the modern mind is difficult to bridge, but not impossible. And those who brave it still find that it is none other than the road to Emmaus on which Jesus' disciples found themselves in conversation about the scriptures with the Resurrected One himself. That road still winds through the modern era, and the conversation with the Lord continues as well. The minds of twenty-first-century travelers may be different from those of first-century ones—as Einstein knew, we cannot live wisely or well with unchanged thinking in a changed and changing world. But the road remains the same and the milestones are familiar ones: regular expectant reading, in touch with community, in dialog with tradition, reason, and experience, followed by quiet listening. These signposts were left by Benedict, Cranmer, and Hooker and are still there for us to follow, even though they have both obstacles and rewards that our forebears did not see. And the goal is the same: theophany, the revelation of God to the likes of us. Happily, our new thinking about scripture can find its footing in the old categories.

Today the road to Emmaus takes us into new territory filled with possibilities and challenges unknown to even the most farsighted of our forebears. In each case, the old markers they left for us, while still valid, have to be extended in order to adequately address the new world in which we find ourselves. In this chapter I will look at scripture, tradition, reason, and experience in order to show how each one must be revisited and built upon to provide this age with the same rich fruit they gave to earlier generations.

scripture revisited

"What then did you go out into the wilderness to see?" Jesus asked the people regarding John the Baptist. The question is a good one for those meeting prophets and for those approaching the Bible. What do you think you have in your hand? A sacred text filled with inerrant mystery? An infallible guide for life, with solutions to particular problems thrown in? Ancient myths and morals only dimly in touch with today's issues? A journalistic account of God's dealing with humankind? Mark Twain, whose piety ran a poor third behind his intellect and wit, wrote that the Bible "is full of interest. It has noble poetry in it and some clever fables; and some blood drenched history; and some good morals and a wealth of obscenity; and upwards of a thousand lies."[11]

Frederick Buechner, whose profound faith is well-known through his many books, is not afraid in all honesty to call the Bible "a disorderly collection of sixty-odd books which are often tedious, barbaric, obscure, and teem with contradictions and inconsistencies. It is a swarming compost of a book, an Irish stew of poetry and propaganda, law and legalism, myth and murk, history and hysteria. Over the centuries it has become hopelessly associated with tub-thumping evangelism and dreary piety, with superannuated superstition and blue-nosed moralizing, with ecclesiastical authoritarianism and crippling literalism." And yet, Buechner continues, because the Bible is "a book about people who at one and the same time can be both believing and unbelieving, innocent and guilty, crusaders and crooks, full of hope and full of despair," it is a book about us, as well as a book about God.[12]

For all the many words that have been written about the Bible, the truth many Christians hold most dear is the simple assertion of hymnist Anna Bartlett Warner, who wrote in 1858 that "Jesus loves me, this I know/ For the Bible tells me so." It is here in the deeper rhythms of the Bible, beneath the roiling surface, that we can come to answer the question of what we come to the Bible to see. As we have noted before, the surface of the Bible is prodigal in its endorsements (slavery, concubinage, polygamy, and capital punishment for unruly children, to name a few) and refuses to make a distinction among prohibitions (wearing tattoos and selling one's daughter into prostitution are side by side in Leviticus 19:28–29). Because it is so uneven it is impossible for the surface—what Hooker called "bare reading" and today we would call literalism—to provide any real coherence. There are those who continue to insist that the surface of the Bible provides an adequate framework for living in spite of its irregularities, but to do so they must also insist that certain texts carry the authority of the Bible in a way that others do not. In my experience those who argue for the authority of the Bible based on the elevation of one or two texts are usually upholding the authority of those who selected the texts, rather than the Bible itself.

While the Bible's surface is a jumble of boisterous contradictions, the deeper, broader principles of revelation afford us a more consistent and valuable resource. Clarity and simplicity remain elusive, as they must whenever we try to grapple with the infinity of God. But it is possible to name some of those basic principles of revelation and to know that whatever we hear God saying, it will be consistent with them. It is possible to name some of the interests of God that give shape and direction to our own decisions and actions. As Christians, we look at scripture through the figure of Jesus, which allows us to sort out some of the chaff the Bible itself does not distinguish. It is what we believe to be the interests of God and what we see in the examples of Jesus that allow us to abhor slavery and take judgments about prostitution more seriously than tattoos.

This short study is not intended to provide a systematic theology of scripture. We can, however, point to a few elements of such a theology. The Bible is a prime source of revelation and as such it provides us with a picture, admittedly sketchy but a picture nonetheless, of God. Something of God's interests can be seen, the heart of God can be gingerly explored, and the will of God is given flashes of clarity.

First of all, the Bible makes it pretty clear that God is all-knowing, all-powerful, and all-loving. God is omniscient and omnipotent love, *agape,* in the language of theologians. We find the expression of these qualities permeates the theology of ancient Israel, the words of the prophets and the psalms, the witness of Jesus, and the faith of the early church. The belief in all three attributes of this love is basic and very important because the exercise of reason alone can let us recognize any two of them but not all three. In our world of hurt and hunger, one could conclude that God knows everything and loves everything but lacks the power to bring it all together into harmony. Or that God has the power but lacks the love, or does not actually know everything that is going on in creation. The Bible insists otherwise, so all that we know of God and all of the trust we place in God are predicated on that revelation.

Second, the creation story in Genesis establishes, and subsequent stories confirm, that God is a "gathering" God. God likes to put things together. Before it all begins the Spirit of God broods over the multi-verse of chaos before bringing the uni-verse of creation into being. That uni-verse is comprised of an intricacy of relationships and consistencies that scientists have only begun to explore. Science could scarcely do its work if 2 plus 2 equals 4 today and 3.7 tomorrow, or if gravity had exceptions, and if only some people had a need for oxygen. God holds the gathered creation together with consistency.

In the Bible's faith story God creates human beings and places them in families, families in clans, clans in tribes, tribes in nations, and calls nations into harmony. In Jesus' day the energy of the faith community had split into factions and strata—Jew and Gentile, Pharisee and Sadducee, clean and unclean, and the categories of sinners were elaborate. Jesus alternately challenged and ignored those distinctions; the healing ministry of Jesus reveals God's interest in putting things back together. This is why our faith story is so full of words like redemption, recon-ciliation, repentance, and renewal. The word "religion" itself literally means "to re-ligament" or "to put back together." The consistent call of Jesus is that we all be one as he and the Father are one. This puts our divisions, segregations, supremacies, nationalism, arrogance, and pride into a harsh light and pushes us toward reconcilia-tion.

Third, God has a particular concern for the lame, the least, and the lost in the human community. Jesus' ministry and teachings underline this fact that is already well-established in the Hebrew scriptures. His mission, he tells us, is to the lost sheep, the blind, and the captive. His continuing presence with us is not in structures, offices, and hierarchies but in "the least" of our brothers and sisters. If the human race were an actual race, God's binoc-ulars would be on the back of the pack, watching over those who are falling behind. God's preoccupation with those who suffer is as clear as anything the Bible tells us about God.

Suggesting that God is revealed to us as all-knowing, all-powerful, and all-loving; as desirous of reconciliation; and as concerned for the suffering and oppressed is not intended to exhaust the Bible's revelation about God, but to indicate that we can identify some of the broader and deeper messages of the Bible. A comprehensive theology of scripture is thus part of the work before us as a church. Without it we will be left to make what sense we can of the choppy irregularities of various texts or, worse, use them as weapons to make people submit to our views and opinions, no matter how enlightened we think they are. The basic principles of the Bible, those that give us the broad-stroke picture of the heart and mind of God, provide illumination of the individual texts and serve as an anchor for the faithful. Our transformed approach to scripture will begin with an understanding of these deeper rhythms.

> Jesus loves me! This I know,
> For the Bible tells me so.
> Little ones to Him belong;
> They are weak, but He is strong.
> Yes, Jesus loves me! Yes, Jesus loves me!
> Yes, Jesus loves me! The Bible tells me so.
> — Anna B. Warner (1827–1915)

One way to begin to get in touch with these Bible basics is to examine the assumptions we are making about God and the Bible, checking to see if they are aligned with what the Bible actually says about God. Scholars tell us that we all have an "embedded theology" made up of our unexamined ideas about life, faith, and God. It is distinct from "deliberative theology"—the ideas we have really worked on and figured out in a systematic way. For example, I have a friend who is a mature and committed Christian. He has given much thought and study to the biblical mandates about meeting the needs of the poor, and his theological position on this issue would be called "deliberative" (think of it as deliberate). When a beloved member of my friend's family had a stroke, his reaction was, "Why did God do this to her when she is such a good person?" This visceral reaction is an example of an embedded theology, growing out of the primitive part of one's faith. On reflection, my friend knew that God, as he knows God, does not go about selecting innocent people for random diseases. A tragic illness exposed his embedded theology and made it clear that it was not in line with the truth revealed in scripture. It got him in touch with one of the deeper rhythms of revelation that our new age requires us to explore.

The Book of Job is another story of people deliberating about their preconceived ideas of God in the face of tragedy. I am not suggesting that we wait patiently for disaster to strike before reflecting on the nature of God. We can, however, imagine ourselves in the role of one of Job's friends, and wonder what we would say if we were called upon to think out loud about a great loss. It is a way of exploring the theology embedded in our own faith. As we look at these assumptions, we will naturally wonder if they are true, solidly based on what scripture reveals. What would you say about God to someone who lost a loved one to an untimely death? What would you say about God to one struggling with addiction or a natural disaster? Do you believe that God causes these things? Is God powerless to prevent them? Maybe God is busy with more important things. Maybe God promised us strength rather than protection. Perhaps God guides us *through* times of trial rather than guides us *away* from them. Is there a difference between a promise to care *for* us and a promise to *take care of us*? What does the Bible actually say about God and people when times are hard? The point is that we can get in touch with those deeper truths by getting a handle on our own assumptions about God and checking them with the biblical realities. Playing the imaginary role of one of Job's friends is one way to revisit scripture.

tradition revisited

The particular value of tradition in our reading of scripture is that it keeps us from the distortions of private faith, the kind of self-serving believing we are all subject to when left to our own devices. Tradition keeps us from fashioning Christianity to suit ourselves. In an essay entitled "On the Reading of Old Books," C. S. Lewis describes it this way:

> Every age has its own outlook. It is especially good at seeing certain truths and especially liable to make certain mistakes. We all, therefore, need the books that will correct the characteristic mistakes of our own period. . . . Not, of course, that there is any magic about the past. People were no cleverer then than they are now; they made as many mistakes as we. But not the same mistakes. . . . Two heads are better than one, not because they are infallible but because they are unlikely to go wrong in the same direction.[13]

Lewis is reminding us of the importance of drawing on the wisdom of those who have gone before us—the "traditional" view of tradition. Lewis, for all of his academic sophistication, was referring to periods and eras of one cultural experience, that of Europe in general and England in particular. The Episcopal Church has as much continuing need of that wisdom as any, but we also have a particular opportunity in being able to draw on streams of tradition that are newly available to us, or more accurately, newly visible to us.

About thirty years ago the Episcopal Church began to value the concept of diversity, to look for it in our congregations and organizations. We established "ethnic desks" at our national headquarters and began to seek diversity in appointments and elections. To me this signified a Spirit-led shift in our life as a faith community. If we remain a one-culture church, our globalizing world will relegate us to a shrinking WASP ghetto—and there is nothing in the gospel that encourages such isolation. The call for diversity in our church sets us on the difficult road of what Ronald Heifetz calls "adaptive change," a basic reordering of our life. Such a change has enormous challenges but we can take at least symbolic comfort in the fact that the Angles and Saxons who gave us the middle two letters of the anagram "WASP" were originally competing tribes, not the monoculture they represent today—and certainly the multiple Protestant denominations in the church today have given evidence of a diversity of church polity and perspectives on the Bible, if nothing else!

The first responses to the call to diversity were cross-cultural—a first step out of the ghetto but only a beginning. Cross-cultural inclusion seeks to bring people into the dominant culture while keeping that culture basically intact—the "melting pot" in which various elements lose their identity and become part of the continuing story of the first group. One of its preoccupying concerns is reaching the tipping point at which the presence of newcomers reaches a significant percentage of the whole so as to change the ongoing life of the dominant culture. This is a frightening prospect because the real motivation of a cross-cultural agenda is to bring others into one's culture, not to allow that culture to be changed. Helping Spanish-speakers to sing English hymns is one thing; including Spanish-language hymns in our worship is quite a different matter. This first step is better than no step at all, but it does not satisfy the call of the Spirit.

The second step is where many of our most progressive dioceses and congregations find themselves today: the various elements of the community are invited in and are encouraged to maintain their identity. Often we have the ideal but not the reality—churches refer to themselves as "diverse congregations" so routinely that the two words are in danger of becoming meaningless. The actual diversity may be the thinnest possible application of a cross-cultural instinct, but the truth is almost always present in the self-portraits of our church.

The problem is that diversity by itself is not a particularly worthy goal. The Reverend Fred Vergara, in his book *Mainstreaming: Asian Americans in the Episcopal Church,* compares this kind of diversity to billiard balls on a table: the balls may roll about, occasionally bumping into each other, but they are not establishing any deeper sense of engagement.[14] If diversity is simply a matter of getting different kinds of people into the same space, it is clear that airports have more diversity than any Episcopal congregation or diocese. So do shopping malls and traffic jams. Those places, of course, have no interest in forming any kind of community out of the diversity, and that second step is where the Episcopal Church faces its challenge. Having an English service and a Spanish service in a single congregation is a fine thing, but without an undergirding sense of community, it is not much more profound than the multilingual murmurings of a crowded security checkpoint at an international airport. Having diverse elements in a diocese or a congregation is a step in the right direction, but our goal is community out of diversity, not simply diversity itself. As with so many other aspects of life in the kingdom of God, diversity is not a stopping place.

The multicultural church can learn much from the New Testament church in Corinth. Saint Paul was dealing with a multicultural congregation with variations in wealth, social background, and spiritual practices. The local methods for dealing with this diversity seem to have relied heavily on bad manners and exclusivity. We should be grateful for the dysfunction of the Corinthian church because Paul's need to straighten them out has given us both the heart of our Eucharistic Prayers ("This is my body that is broken for you...This cup is the new covenant in my blood" [1 Corinthians 11:23–26]). and the wonderful hymn to love ("If I speak in the tongues of mortals and of angels, but do not have love" [1 Corinthians 13]). But his first letter to the Corinthians has also provided a "hymn to diversity," in which Paul speaks of many gifts and one body: "Now there are varieties of gifts, but the same Spirit.... For in the one Spirit we were all baptized into one body—Jews or Greeks, slaves or free—and we were all made to drink of one Spirit" (1 Corinthians 12). His point is that the gifts of the Spirit in all their diversity are meant to find their fullness in relationship to one another, and that is what leads us beyond multiculturalism to interculturalism.

Indeed, the body does not consist of one member but of many. If the foot would say, "because I am not a hand, I do not belong to the body," that would not make it any less a part of the body.... God arranged the members in the body, each one of them, as he chose. If all were a single member, where would the body be? As it is, there are many members, yet one body. (1 Corinthians 12:14–20)

Interculturalism is a new order brought into being by the gathering of many cultures, or in the categories Hooker gave us, many *traditions*. Some like the image of a salad bowl to describe it; my personal preference is of a gumbo, but the idea is the same. Unlike the melting pot, where each element disappears into the dominant strain, or the pool table, where different balls clack into one another, here the various pieces make a new whole, with each piece still identifiable but altered, seasoned and enriched by the mix. In this new mix the several traditions that have shaped the diverse elements of our church remain distinct but form a whole new reality. Theologian Mark McDonald highlights the meaning of interculturalism when he writes, "In the various facets of the Gospel life and light, refracted in the living experience of peoples renewed in Christ, we begin to see the first rays of a dawning for the new humanity intended for the Church."[15] This new understanding of tradition will be ready to illuminate, animate, and enliven our reading of scripture when we follow the leading of the Holy Spirit beyond cross-culturalism through multiculturalism toward interculturalism.

But how do we get ready for it? Congregations are self-selecting volunteer bodies. While some of us actively seek the stimulation and challenges of other cultures in our worshipping life, most of us look for the comfort that comes from like-minds. And there are many in our church who could not have a significant cross-cultural, multicultural, or intercultural experience if they wanted to. Several years ago I served on a county Human Rights Commission in my native West Virginia. The non-white population of our county added up to less than one percent. Insofar as culture is expressed by color, we did not have many options. Times have undoubtedly changed the scene, but it is not fair to assume that everyone has ready access to cultures other than their own. Geography is one factor; our place in history is another. There are many communities and congregations who have never given a moment's thought to what other cultures might have to offer them and vice versa. It is literally a foreign concept. No one is responsible for what was done or not done by the generations that preceded them and there is little to be gained by wondering why they did or did not. As Winston Churchill famously warned, if we let the past and the present argue we will lose the future. And it is on the future that our eyes need to be set.

The gathering God, who from Genesis to Generation X has been calling diverse people and communities together, is still at it. Are you wondering how you might be part of that calling? Can you imagine how your congregation might join in it? You will have to start from where you are, whether it is an urban mix or a small homogeneous community. "Wonder" is a good place to start. It is the beginning of the itch. It raises the questions that will open our eyes to see the doors that God is opening. "Wonder" can be sharpened with reading and, where possible, conversations with those of differing traditions. The Episcopal Church is being offered a great source of enrichment through the various traditions of Anglicanism that are flowing around and through us.

---

reason revisited

In Mark McDonald's writings on the value of interculturalism, he states that, "Since the Enlightenment, the churches of the West have tended to limit God's activity and presence within the explicit realm of church belief, teaching and practice."[16] While one might debate the extent to which such a statement is true, it does seem to apply to the manner in which Richard Hooker understood the exercise of reason in what was later termed the three-legged stool of Anglicanism. For Hooker, reason was focused on scripture, which is pretty well identified with the realm of the church. He was concerned that Anglicans have not only the freedom but an eagerness to think critically about a text. His opponents were the literalists of his day, who insisted that the true meaning of the Bible lay on the surface for the faithful readily to see. They regarded what later generations dubbed "biblical criticism" as heretical. Hooker thought it was essential. Since the Puritans of Hooker's day are wearing different uniforms but are still among us now, the importance of his argument stands but it needs to be expanded.

In Hooker's sixteenth century, science as we know it was embryonic and posed few problems for Bible-reading Christians. The relatively narrow focus to which McDonald refers was a reasonable allocation of the forces of reason. Such is not the case today. Many find their faith rattled and even destroyed by the issues raised by scientific inquiry and discovery. The faith position that is particularly vulnerable to science has been called a belief in a "God of the Gaps," meaning that God is found only in the gaps in human knowledge, in phenomena that cannot be explained and are, therefore, attributable to God. As our knowledge of the world expanded, the gaps became fewer and God-sightings dependent on those gaps became more rare. Although the current debates about creationism have not played a major role in the Episcopal Church because we are less tied to the literalist view that wants Genesis to be a science book as well as a revelation of the heart of God and the meaning of life, the concerns of the creationists provide a ready illustration of a "God of the Gaps" theology. Creationists maintain that indications of natural processes, such as evolution, diminish the image of a God who is mindfully directing the course of the universe. "Where science speaks, God is silenced" might be a motto of this theology. The flower of God's reign must be protected from the harsh light of scientific inquiry lest it wither and die. This was the view of the church when Copernicus and Galileo found that the earth revolved around the sun instead of vice versa. It is the view of those Christians who want Darwin kept on a leash, along with various archeologists, paleontologists, geologists, and astronomers.

While most Episcopalians view the Genesis versus science struggle with bemused indifference, there is another effort that is required of us. If we distance ourselves from a "God of the Gaps" theology, what position do we take? If we do not join our co-religionists in resisting the inroads of natural science into the old prerogatives of God, what do we think *are* the prerogatives of God today? Where do we see God at work? What on earth does God do? Does the expansion of human knowledge necessarily encroach on the habitat of God the same way that expanding cities encroach of the habitat of bears and beavers? Are we forced back into the position of the Deists, who maintained that God created the laws of nature and then stepped back—way back, out of reach and out of touch—to let them run? If not, then we Episcopalians have some responsibility for recasting the relationship between science and religion. That renegotiated relationship is on the forefront of the new challenge to our powers of what Hooker called reason.

Almighty and everlasting God, you made the universe with all its marvelous order, its atoms, worlds, and galaxies, and the infinite complexity of living creatures: Grant that, as we probe the mysteries of your creation, we may come to know you more truly, and more surely fulfill our role in our eternal purpose. *— The Book of Common Prayer*

As we learn how to approach and use scripture in the current age, we will be speaking to a culture that is fascinated by and dependent upon the works of science. This is not the definitive book on scientific inquiry and scriptural integrity, but when that book is written I think it will include these points. First, the Bible does not need to be protected from inquiry in any form. It has been said that the truth is like a torch: the more you shake it, the brighter it becomes. The light of truth that shines on the Bible does not diminish the truth that shines from it, and vice versa. This means that we need not fear or hold as inherently "counter-Christian" any area of research and learning. It does mean that we will need a firm grip on the unchanging realities of God, the aforementioned deeper rhythms and truths of scripture, because every question is good but every answer is not. We can encourage scientific research into cloning without forfeiting our concept of life as God-given. We can explore the wisdom of Islam and the Qu'ran in a way that enriches our Christianity. We can discuss immigration while holding the value as well as the distinction between what is legal and what is just. We can do all of these things and more if—and this is a big "if"—we can distinguish the unchanging facts of our faith from its constantly changing expressions and applications. The "bare reading" of the text will not help us: when Genesis 1:26 tells us that people are to have dominion over creation and subdue it, while Genesis 2:16 tells us that we are to till the ground and keep it, we will end up with very different approaches to the environment. Speaking to a different issue, Roman Catholic scholar Gilbert Meilaender rightly distinguished between the surface and the heart of scripture in saying, "We cannot claim . . . that the Bible itself establishes the point at which individual life begins, although it surely directs our attention to the value of fetal life."[17] Of course, a great deal of this research science will be done well over my head and probably yours, but we need not fear the questions nor discourage those who wrestle with them.

Second, the exercise of religion is one of unifying. As we have seen, the word itself means literally "to put back together," to "re-ligament." Too often those who represent this unifying force have turned it into a suppressing force and in so doing have failed to practice its tenets while also failing to keep truth from finding ways to express itself. Moses stopped and faced the burning bush because he did not understand it. Similarly, we must stop and face the phenomena and discoveries we do not understand, expecting the Holy Spirit to continue to guide us along the path of truth. It may be that the most dynamic field of theological inquiry is theoretical physics or genome research.

Third, "panentheism" is a theological mouthful but it is a principle we will want to develop and rely upon. Briefly stated, it is the idea that God is in everything. It differs from the slightly more familiar term "pantheism," which means that everything *is* God and God is the sum of everything that is. That one is a heresy, which means that it is not quite true enough to be taken seriously. Pan-en-theism (literally "all-in-god") is different in that it acknowledges the presence of the Creator in everything created. Psalm 139 makes this point with its poignant questions: "Where can I go then from your Spirit? where can I flee from your presence? If I climb up to heaven, you are there; if I make the grave my bed, you are there also" (139:6–7, BCP). The Book of Jeremiah also touches on it when God asks, "Who can hide in secret places so that I cannot see them? says the LORD. Do I not fill heaven and earth? says the LORD" (Jeremiah 23:24). It lies behind the miracle story of Pentecost, when the Holy Spirit was poured out "upon all flesh," thus fulfilling the prophecy in the Book of Joel concerning the time when "everyone who calls on the name of the Lord shall be saved" (Acts 2:1–21). What makes panentheism so important is that it sets us at the task of integrating the discoveries of the sciences into our theology rather than warring against them.

Fourth and last, such an integration will change our theology, just as interculturalism will change our church. Our brightest and best minds will be needed to guide the transformation. We will need new and keen eyes to help us keep our sense of the eternal intact as the temporal expressions of it change rapidly. We will have to keep the changeable symbols of truth distinct from the truths themselves. Our spiritual ancestors had to learn how to sing the Lord's song in a world made strange by change—by the new realities of the destruction of Jerusalem, the acceptance of Gentiles, critical readings of Genesis, and theories concerning the evolution of the species. Our generation will be singing it in the context of cloning, global warming, the rise of Islam, and stem cell research. The Episcopal Church, inheritor of the intellectual agility of the Thirty-nine Articles and Richard Hooker, is in a better place than most Christian traditions to do this vital work.

experience revisited

In chapter two I suggested that the ultimate goal of Bible study is theophany, the experience of revelation—hearing God speak, feeling God's pull, knowing God's presence. Is it unfair to say that many of us in the Episcopal Church are not so different from the Deists of the eighteenth century, who maintained that God established nature's laws and then retired to an undisclosed location? Are there solid creed-sayers, pledge-payers, hymn-singers, and communion-taking churchgoers who neither expect nor experience God in their lives? The churches I know are full of them, and if that also matches your experience, it explains why the whole idea of "experience" must be revisited.

The fact is, God is present, not absent. It has been said that religion is living as if God were present and secularism is living as if God were absent. There may be some, even many, of us who wear religious garb over secular hearts, but that does not change God. The reality is the same one that the orthodox of the eighteenth century affirmed: God's is present in the world and can be known through experience.

According to panentheism, there is no part of creation in which God is not found, sustaining the life of each element. In the beautiful prologue to John's gospel, we are told that all things came into being through God and that God remains the "light of all people." Paul's letter to the Colossians makes that point even clearer by asserting that "in him all things hold together" (1:17). It is not unreasonable to wonder how God might be actually present in a human life. At one time many of us worshipped a "God of the Gaps," who dwelt in the mysteries between and beyond our understandings, but such a god is helplessly squeezed by scientific knowledge as well as cynicism, frustration, and secular mythologies, such as, "It does not matter what you believe as long as you are sincere," or "God has more to do than worry about me." Yet God is present in ways that all of us know even if we cannot actually define them.

When I was a young boy my family said that I had many of the traits of my grandfather. I did not look like him, but I sounded like him and even had a habit of walking with my hands behind my back as he did. He died when I was five. How did his traits get into me? Imitation? DNA? Who knows—or cares? Am I somehow less of myself because I include some of him, because he is in some way "in me"? Of course not. But in some mysterious way my grandfather dwells within me.

In a similar way, anyone who has watched a child grow up has seen the Creator's hand at work. In children we can see so clearly the set stages of development through which each child passes, with more or less set times for certain skills, interests, discoveries, and pursuits. At one point fingers and toes are discovered; at another time, sexuality. At one age the repetition of slow-turning ceiling fans is fascinating; later on, the same favorite stories will be asked for over and over. In a few years a child's love of repetition will be replaced by the inconsistencies of the teen years: relationships with parents are negotiated at one age and renegotiated later. All of these things are predictable, yet every child walks that path in a style all his or her own. How much comes from the parents, how much from the child's own nature, and how much from God dwelling within? These distinct realities work together in a human life without being compromised or diminished in any way. We do not know exactly how God is present in our lives any more than we understand how a baby knows when it is time to crawl or why a young boy walks like his grandfather, but God dwells in our lives and in all of creation even if we cannot find the actual boundary between them.

Surely the LORD is in this place—and I did not know it!...How awesome is this place! This is none other than the house of God, and this is the gate of heaven.
(Genesis 28:16–17)

The most pressing question for us is not God's presence but the *experience* of that presence. I have no separate experience of my grandfather as I continue to walk with my hands behind my back. Children have no particular experience of the Creator as they move from ceiling fans to dances. But these are only analogies for experiencing God. How do we know the real thing?

There is a positive response to that question even though there can never be an answer. God is not "on call" for us, and we must beware of formulas that promise us an experience of the living God. Nonetheless, there are places we can go, things we can do, attitudes we can adopt that will make an encounter with God more likely, but that is as much as one can say. It has been famously said that the island of Iona, where Saint Columba based his mission to Scotland, is a "thin place," meaning that the separation between heaven and earth is less pronounced. There are many such places in the world and in our own memories where we are most likely to be aware of God. Churches, retreat centers, places of quiet beauty, reflective places come to mind. But God remains full of surprises, popping up when we least expect and disappearing when we most desire. Reading the Bible is more likely to bring us into contact with God's Word than *Popular Mechanics* or *The Wall Street Journal,* but it does not always happen with the former and we cannot say it never happens with the latter. The stories of the great mystics and saints of our faith are full of empty stretches where neither determination nor discipline could bring God into focus for them.

With all of that firmly in mind, let us consider a tool that has proven to be both accessible and fruitful for the ordinary Christian. The tool is another theological mouthful: it is known as "cultural hermeneutic," which refers to the study and interpretation of religious texts through the lens of a particular cultural experience. One well-known example of this is the field of liberation theology, a Roman Catholic approach to theology from "below," through the plight of the poor and the marginalized, who are especially favored by God. Offering a stinging critique of both society and the church, liberation theology arose from the social turmoil of the 1960s and 1970s in Latin America, where both leaders and peasants began to read the Bible from this perspective. They did not just ask what the Bible said in any given text, but what it specifically said about the poor and to the poor. Oscar Romero was but one of its exemplars. The scriptural assurances of God's special care for the downtrodden, the radical promises of upheaval in the lovely *Magnificat* of Mary, and the whole story of the Exodus and wilderness experience became a source of life and hope. This interpretation provided great positive energy for the reforms and the reformers at work in the church, the government, and the community at large.

The insights of liberation theology were soon picked up by others. This principle of holding an intentional point of view—reading the Bible through the lens of a particular set of issues—began to be applied by people whose concerns were not poverty, but other kinds of marginalization, whether because of gender, race, sexual orientation, or aging. People found that if some passionate issue was brought to the biblical text, the Bible itself came crackling to life. The principle is not new, of course, but liberation theology and those in its circle of influence found new ways to bridge the gap between the ancient and modern worlds. The Episcopal Church in the twenty-first century will want to incorporate the best practices of cultural hermeneutics as we read, mark, learn, and inwardly digest the words of scripture.

There is a fine and somewhat dangerous line between this practice and proof-texting, or finding the verses that support your thesis. As I said earlier, the Bible is like a person—if you torture it long enough you can get it to say almost anything. Following this path is a way of listening to God, not using God as your proxy lawyer. The integrity of the liberation theologians enabled them to hear the Word of the Lord rather than an echo of their own minds.

Any person of faith can bring the compelling issues of life to the biblical meeting ground. We can read the Bible with the appalling consequences of the unequal distribution of the world's wealth on our hearts, or turn to it with questions that are more intimate and personal—health, relationships, decisions, fear, hope, grief, anxiety, and faith. You may recall that my first experience of hearing God speak through scripture was based on my panic over reading in public. My fear gave me a point of view that made a major difference in what I "heard" in the appointed psalm. The trick is to articulate the concern or issue and then listen for what God might say about it through scripture. All of the disciplines of study, community discernment, and connecting the original meaning of the text to the present time remain vital so that we do not become "rootless," as Archbishop Williams has cautioned. But the Bible does still speak with God's own voice, and people like you and me can still hear it.

As I thought about trying to use a disciplined hermeneutic of my own in my personal devotional life, I tried an experiment that has proven to be very helpful and affirmed for me the value of this approach. My daily discipline is a form of Morning Prayer that follows the Prayer Book outline of focusing, reading the appointed lessons, and ending with prayer. It has "worked" for me for many years, as it has for countess others over the centuries. My experiment was to *reverse* the sequence of readings and prayers. I found that the prayers focused my mind on the things my heart normally carries—big issues like poverty and war, the direction of our country and our church; more personal issues like the health of a loved one, a decision, or a relationship. The prayers gave me some clarity about the miniculture that is my own little world. Those matters became the hermeneutic I applied to the Bible. In that context, when I followed the collect's advice to "hear, read, mark, learn, and inwardly digest" the scripture readings, my experience of God increased tenfold.

My little exercise lacks any of the credibility of a survey or something that has stood the test of time. It does have the advantage of being quite portable from my experience to your own, and requires only a slight tweaking of the ancient pattern of Morning Prayer. The point is that God is present and engaged in creation. Scripture is one of the places where we can, as our spiritual ancestors have done for millennia, experience God and hear God's Word to us as a way of finding guidance in the times we need it most.

The common lament in our era is that we do not have time for regular reading of the Bible. That is not true, of course, but this excuse is so widely accepted that we forget that it is a way of evading a truth we don't want to accept: that everybody has the same amount of time. Days are a standard twenty-four hours. No one has more or less; none of us lacks time for Bible reading. What we do not have is a priority for Bible reading. We do what we think it is important to do. I have no doubt that our days are spent dealing with things of genuine importance and of a compelling nature. The question is whether regular reading of the Bible could work its way into that schedule. The answer is it probably will not, unless we see a clear value in doing so. What if we really thought there was a better-than-average chance we would experience the living God by doing it? What if we tried reading the Bible expectantly, as a way of meeting the Lord in scripture and understanding our most passionate concerns, just as many people have been doing for four thousand years? Would that discipline conceivably move higher and higher on our list of priorities for the day?

Stories from the Meeting Ground

When I was in college, a variety of factors combined to lead me to look at my faith in different ways. My experiences in the world around me and the fresh deposits of my new ways of thinking cried out for some kind of glue to hold it all together. I did not know then that the word "religion" literally means "to put back together," but I did know enough to expect my faith to do just that. The chaplain on campus listened with grace to my ramblings and gave me what was then a hot-off-the-press copy of the New English Bible. It was so new that only the New Testament was available, but it was enough to start me down a path of discovery that has given me joy and wonder from that day to this.

I was an English major, so I spent a lot of time reading books of one kind or another. I studied them, outlined them, took tests on them, wrote essays about them, enjoyed them, and was sometimes bored to tears by them. But I had never had a conversation with one. This New English Bible, a translation not widely used today, was a revelation to me. It spoke to me about *me,* and invited me to speak back. I wrote all over it, marking places that confused me, putting stars by the lines that jumped out at me, arguing with what seemed to be absurdities, and wandering around the places I would later think of as the "meeting ground" where God is so often heard.

I did not know it then, but I was not alone in that time of discovery, and I remain in good company now. Throughout the ages, countless men and women have heeded scripture's invitation to conversation. Today in thousands and thousands of homes, study groups, chapels, websites, prayer circles, and quiet places people are experiencing the inexhaustible riches of the Bible. Yet, as you know, biblical knowledge in the Episcopal Church remains irregular and uneven. In spite of a heritage that has been fed by the early storytellers, shaped by monks, deepened by scholars, challenged by failures, and enriched by theophanies, and in spite of wonderful resources from Alpha to EfM, many in our church reflect Thomas Bray's three-hundred-year-old concern: they are "utterly destitute" of biblical knowledge, and "in want of instruction" in the Christian faith. That remains a lamentable part of the truth about our church, but it is far from the whole truth. In this chapter I will share some of the stories of congregations, dioceses, and ministries in our church that have been enriched, transformed, and shaped by creative engagement with God's Word.

multicultural listening

One of God's gifts to the twenty-first century church is the opportunity to learn from the faith experiences of diverse peoples and cultures. Gospel Based Discipleship, the discipline that we considered earlier in chapter three of listening for personal and communal messages in a text, is "a way of life in the Diocese of Alaska." More an encounter with the gospel than a study-based approach to it, Gospel Based Discipleship incorporates wisdom and traditions that are rooted in Native American experience. It is used in almost every Alaskan congregation as part of the work of vestries, spiritual formation groups, and prayer groups. On the diocesan level it holds the center in the work of committees and commissions, the annual diocesan convention, and in the discernment processes of the Commission on Ministry.

The three basic questions of Gospel Based Discipleship—What stands out for you? What is the gospel saying to you? What is it calling you to do?—mean that people gather with the expectation that Jesus is present and will teach them.

They gather in what Alaska calls "a circle of love," a small group that seeks to be together as Jesus would have us be together, honestly and openly. Multiple readings of the gospel appointed for the day are considered in the light of the three questions. As part of the ministry discernment process, moreover, aspirants form a special Gospel Based Discipleship group where the questions are changed to focus on the call to ministry: "What is the gospel saying about this call to ministry? and "What does it say should be done?" At diocesan conventions, Gospel Based Discipleship is used as Morning Prayer, with people gathering sometimes in assigned groups and sometimes in random ones. In an interesting expansion of Robert's Rules of Order, at any point in the meeting of the diocese a member may call for a reading of the day's gospel. "This has been very effective when we get 'stuck' on something," says Ginny Doctor, Alaska's Canon to the Ordinary. She recounts one story where a group was struggling to understand a vision for their work and encountering sharp divisions as to what that vision might be. A reading of the gospel was called for, and in the circle the text spoke with clarity about the desired direction. The argument ended and the group followed the gospel lead. "I am always amazed," says Doctor, "how the gospel of the day fits into whatever I am doing."

Others in the church are practicing Gospel Based Discipleship as well, allowing dynamic encounter with the scriptures beyond Alaska. On the Island of Guam in the Diocese of Micronesia, for example, such groups meet on Thursday mornings to prepare for Sunday worship. The benefit is a richer Sunday experience and deepening spiritual relationships among the participants. The Diocese of North Carolina has also prepared a Gospel Based Discipleship outline for use by individuals, groups, retreat participants, and as part of Morning Prayer. It includes Gospel Based Discipleship's guiding questions, suggested prayers, a diocesan intercessory prayer list, and a year-long lectionary of gospel readings.

When the disciplines of patience and Christ-centered conversation are applied to the Bible, even the most energetic and fidgety of Christians can experience its power. Brian Prior of the Diocese of Spokane is a clerical youth advisor for Province VIII. He tells of using a Gospel Based Discipleship approach to guide teenagers' preparation for a major youth event. After three slow, reflective readings in which the planning group followed the Gospel Based Discipleship questions, the young people were asked what they believed God was calling them to bring to their peers at the event. Lively discussion led them to their programmatic theme, which was then reduced to a separate word or phrase for each day of the gathering. At the beginning of the youth event itself, the full gospel text was introduced verbally, dramatically, and with multimedia. Each day was built on its particular gospel word, and the culminating service returned the participants to the full text. The kind of thoughtful building on a biblical text that the Province VIII teenagers accomplished can lend grace and an experience of the Holy Spirit to any church gathering.

As one participant observed, "I've heard that Bible story a hundred times but this experience made it come alive for me."

One of the opportunities the twenty-first century affords Anglicanism is an expanded concept of tradition. Whereas in the past we took tradition to mean the European experience filtered through England, now it includes a convergence of European, African, African American, Asian, Hispanic, and Native American experiences. Our ability to draw upon this richness will greatly determine our success in becoming a truly intercultural church. The wide and varied uses of Gospel Based Discipleship provide an opportunity for the familiar stories to come alive in ways our forebears could not have imagined.

---

the Bible in the midst of conflict

The Bible, whether read in sacred circles or private study, speaks most clearly when its readers are keenly aware of a need to be addressed. Times of anxiety, tension, and crisis have a way of sharpening our hearing by focusing the sense of expectation that is so basic to vital Bible reading. The recent controversies in the Episcopal Church have seen the Bible used in many ways. Some have been destructive, such as biased proof-texting, highly selective reading of scripture, and attempts to prove that a text does not say what it says. But many others have been faithful and constructive, as people worked to follow the Spirit's leading into all truth, wrestled with deeper meanings, and struggled with priorities in apparently conflicting texts and interpretations. Here are three among the many stories of healthy and positive uses of scripture in conflict situations.

The Diocese of the Rio Grande has been clear in its understanding of the issues around human sexuality. As is often the case in dioceses with such clarity, no matter what position they are clear about, non-juring congregations are to be found. St. Michael and All Angels in Albuquerque is often at odds with the diocesan leadership on this and other issues. In 1996 the parish was growing and in need of additional space. A $1 million project was developed, with a substantial low-interest loan from the diocese as an important element. The continuing active ministry of St. Michael's in the gay and lesbian community caused the diocesan leadership to reconsider its support for the expansion project and the loan offer was withdrawn. The congregation was required to seek a commercial loan at a substantially higher rate of interest. The people of St. Michael's were frustrated and angry over the diocesan decision. Some felt there had been a breach of promise and that the congregation should sue. Several parish-wide meetings were held, with the possibility of a lawsuit openly discussed. The rector, Brian Taylor, recounts this moment in one of the meetings:

> What happened was a movement of the Spirit, a manifestation of God's grace among us. Jim Tyron, our senior warden, a faithful and prayerful man, stood among our people and reminded them that we are people of the gospel. Jesus called us again and again to forgive our enemies, to turn the other cheek, to not return evil for evil. When Jim dropped these well-known gospel truths into the midst of our pain, it was like placing a gigantic mirror in front of us all. We saw ourselves in the light of the gospel. For the first time for many of us it occurred to us, as one parishioner put it, that "Jesus really meant what he said about forgiveness. This is not some abstract idea. It is right here, right

now, and we have a choice as to whether we are going to be faithful to Christ."

The parish did not sue, but sought to model faithful behavior in the diocese and in their continuing ministry among homosexual persons. The commercial loan was paid in full, just three years later.

When Jim dropped these well-known gospel truths into the midst of our pain, it was like placing a gigantic mirror in front of us all. We saw ourselves in the light of the gospel. For the first time for many of us it occurred to us, as one parishioner put it, that "Jesus really meant what he said about forgiveness."
—Brian Taylor, St. Michael and All Angels Church

My two other examples of the Bible being used faithfully in situations of tension are both about systems in which the authors have taken a clear position on a subject and offer appropriate biblical support for that position. They have different positions in regard to the specific issues currently before us, but they share a common respect for scripture as a vital source of grounding and guidance. Together they illustrate a continuing conundrum in the church: good people of faith and reason can come to very different conclusions about the implications of biblical texts.

In 2006 several non-juring congregations in the Diocese of Virginia were struggling with their relationship with the Episcopal Church, and a booklet entitled *40 Days of Discernment* was prepared for use during that time. The unnamed authors stated clearly their conviction that the Episcopal Church was in such grievous error that the burden of proof was on those who wished to remain in its community. They thought that "the real question is not whether but how unity will break." The booklet contains resources for forty days of individual or group study. It is seriously rooted in scripture and is intended to be carried out in a context of both prayer and fasting. There is a brief piece on the practice and role of fasting for those unfamiliar with it. All in all, this study aid aims to bring together the catholic and evangelical streams in Anglicanism, with its emphasis on serious Bible study along with classic Christian spiritual disciplines.

The 2004 Windsor Report was commissioned by the Archbishop of Canterbury to examine, among other things, the implications of electing and consecrating Gene Robinson as bishop of New Hampshire. It asked the question, "How can someone living in a same-sex union be eligible to lead the flock of Christ?" The response was prepared by a team of seven scholars under the title *To Set Our Hope on Christ*. In addition to its thoughtful formal response to the request of the Windsor Commission, it includes a thorough appendix delineating the General Convention studies and decisions on this matter, stretching back forty years. Although not widely known in either the Episcopal Church or the Anglican Communion, this short volume (sixty pages of text, seventy pages of appendix) sets the story of our church and the decisions of 2003 firmly in the wider context of the biblical narrative as it has been understood in the Anglican tradition. The journey of our church is interpreted in light of the painful and course-changing decision of the church in Jerusalem to include Gentiles in the Christian fellowship (see Acts 10:15). It is a gracious and well-reasoned biblical, theological, and ethical case. Neither *To Set Our Hope on Christ* nor *40 Days of Discernment* will convince everyone, but together they do show how the Bible can be a solid base even as Episcopalians struggle with our various understandings of that base.

On a much smaller and gentler scale, the Reverend Suzanne Guthrie introduced the practice of "pretending the Bible" while serving in children's ministries at Holy Cross Church in Kingston, New York. Grade-school and middle-school students gathered on Monday evenings for Christian education. When a story was read, the class was asked to list all of the possible roles, including inanimate objects, such as walls or golden calves, or natural phenomena, like wind. Once the parts of the story were named, students chose one or more roles as their own and donned costumes representing, in the broadest possible way, the chosen role. The story was then "pretended," with students working out the actions and relationships of the several parts. The result was never a skit or performance, but an entering into the story in which everyone participated. Afterward they put away the costumes and talked about what each had noticed during the pretending.

The depth at which the children appropriated the stories was well-illustrated during a visit to a local Jewish temple. Guthrie reports that the class immediately "recognized the twelve stones on the door of the tabernacle. 'Look, Aaron's breastplate! Which jewel is which? Which one is Gad? Asher? Naphtali?' The kids went on and on. (They even knew that Ephraim and Manasseh were the children of Joseph and not Jacob.) The rabbi was shocked that these elementary-school-age Christian children from Kingston knew the tribes of Israel. I was surprised too, but they had never 'learned' the tribes by rote. We had just pretended the stories."

While pretending the Bible may be a little unconventional, traditional parish-based Bible study groups still hold sway in our church and continue to make a profound difference in people's lives. Ellis Brazeal attended such a group at the Cathedral Church of the Advent in Birmingham, Alabama. Ellis is a lawyer who lives in a world with high expectations for himself, his colleagues, and his family. Meeting those demands was the agenda of every day, the heart of every relationship, and the foundation of every hope he had of salvation. Paul Zahl, dean of the cathedral, was the Bible study leader and the man who was able to hold Brazeal still long enough for the radical, world-shaking truth of the gospel to take hold. "Each week the Bible was brought alive," Brazeal writes, "and I came to grips with who I was—a sinner—and who God is—a redeemer of sinners.... As I learned that God had no expectations for me (or, more properly, that Christ had satisfied them on the cross), I began to remove expectations from my wife and children.... God powerfully used this Bible study to draw me to Christ, which wrought a transformation in me which blessed my wife, children, friends and others." Ellis's wife, Debbie, agrees that their marriage moved from danger to joy because of the radical gospel message heard in the Thursday morning Bible study at the cathedral.

Each week the Bible was brought alive, and I came to grips with who I was—a sinner—and who God is—a redeemer of sinners.... God powerfully used this Bible study to draw me to Christ, which wrought a transformation in me which blessed my wife, children, friends, and others. — *Ellis Brazeal, Cathedral Church of the Advent*

Sometimes the Bible comes alive through theological reflection and sometimes through personal reflection. The Reverend Sarabeth Goodwin, a Latino missioner in the Diocese of Washington (D.C.), works with a largely Mexican immigrant community based at St. Stephen and the Incarnation Church. The congregants' backgrounds are almost exclusively Roman Catholic and include very little acquaintance with the Bible, especially the Hebrew scriptures. To fill this gap, a Lenten study focused on the great early archetypal stories, including the Exodus and the wandering in the wilderness.

The lay leader asked if the group members could imagine what it would be like to wander in the desert. As with many such gatherings, the group included undocumented workers. One told a story of a long trek to the border where the "coyote," the one who would lead them across, told her that she was too heavy to make the long journey through the desert. The storyteller said she was not about to quit at that point and insisted on making the crossing. Someone in the group asked her how she managed to make it. She answered that a fine mist settled in the area for the two days she walked in the wilderness, so she was able to endure the heat. There was an awed silence as the group considered the wonder of such a thing. The spell was broken when a man with only one year of formal education provided the words of revelation: "Manna in the desert," he said. All nodded, recognizing the wisdom that makes connections between our stories and the great stories of the Bible. The group went on to share other stories of God's providence touching their lives in desert places and times of wandering.

The Bible often speaks most powerfully to those who are not tempted to miss its message by over-intellectualizing. The Episcopal chaplaincy at Cornell University in Ithaca, New York, has known many successes in accompanying people on their spiritual journeys, but, like many such ministries, has not done particularly well with Bible studies. Perhaps students have trouble shifting from the way they study Toni Morrison or William Faulkner to the way they study the Bible, but for whatever reason, the path to Bible study groups is not well-worn on most college campuses. The students at Cornell, however, did have an opportunity to experience the power of scripture through their ministry at a young women's detention center. Jessie DeGrado was one of the students involved and tells the story of the weekly Bible study at the facility. In the fall of 2006 they began meeting with five or six young girls in "the ugliest room ever," under the watchful eye of guards, in the glare of neon lights, sitting on "horrible institutional couches." In that setting, as unlikely as Jacob's troubled wilderness dream on a stone pillow, the Spirit hovered and moved, making the space almost "cozy." The format was simple: check in, a collect, a psalm and the gospel for the day, discussion, a closing prayer. Jessie was aware of the girls' need for the Bible's message of forgiveness and love supported by the one-on-one attention of the Cornell missioners. The wonder of the experience drew heavily on the young women's fearless questioning of the Bible. Basic questions of chronology and complex questions about heaven and hell shed light in the room with or without clear answers. The girls' ease with extemporaneous prayer "had me totally beat," admits Jessie, and their insight into texts was remarkable. During a discussion of John 17, the high priestly prayer that is considered theologically challenging by most scholars, they paused at verse 21, which reads in part, "As you, Father, are in me and I am in you, may they also be in us." "Look!" exclaimed one of the girls. "We're being invited into the Trinity! This is so exciting—I can be part of the Trinity." And so, having found her place in the kingdom of heaven, this young woman returned to her earthly cell.

a storytelling church

As we have seen, Episcopalians have all of the pieces in place for a powerful experience with the Bible—so why are we not characterized by such experiences? I would suggest that our immunity comes from the fact that not enough of us have allowed the disciplines of good Bible reading to become a priority in our lives. The beginning question is, therefore, how can we get Episcopalians to make room in their day for regular, expectant reading of the Word?

It will not be easy. Whatever we do takes all day. Everybody is busy with something. Few of us have time-consuming habits that are obviously evil and need to be rooted out of our schedules, thereby making room for Bible study. For fruitful Bible listening to happen, something worthwhile has to be set aside. Why would anyone make such a change? Perhaps because someone they respect told them of the value of such a discipline. The methods and systems described in chapter three are only a few of the many programs in use today. They have thousands upon thousands of adherents. What would happen if the people who practice them began to tell others what meaning and value they find in their engagement with the Bible?

As with many good words, "evangelism" has been ripped from its root meaning and allowed to become something it should not be. The word literally means "storytelling," and evangelism in its true form is simply sharing part of one's story, telling another person about something that has meaning for us. In this way it is not different from what we do when we find a bargain at the mall or a movie we enjoy. It does not require great training or courage to tell others about those things; could we not do the same with Bible reading? Those who have been to the meeting ground and have heard the still, clear voice that has the power to reassure, hasten, and guide our lives might consider telling others about that voice, and those others just might begin to rearrange their priorities to include trips to that meeting ground.

This simple step does not require us to invent a new program or learn a new language. All we need to do is apply to scripture what we already apply to new recipes, the cute things our children say, and our political opinions: *tell someone.* We who know the value of Bible listening need only let go of our reluctance to mention anything about our spiritual life. It requires us to make a distinction between that which is personal and that which is private, acknowledging that our life before God is the former but not the latter. Our faith assumes sharing and relies upon it. The Judeo-Christian tradition would have died with Abraham and Sarah if their descendants had not remembered and passed along their story to others, who also knew the same God—the One who likewise calls us into the wilderness and into new life.

Once interest has been piqued and the vitality of scripture has been shared, we have many fruitful resources at hand. Different people will be drawn to different points of entry. All other things being equal, however, I would suggest some form of the African Bible study method would be a good introduction to the meeting ground. As you may recall, one criticism of this method is that in and of itself it does not include any form of study. Study is indeed vital if we are to encounter the deep riches of the Bible, but it is not the best starting place. The African Bible study method provides a way of experiencing the Bible's capacity to speak to our lives by seeing the Word emerge from the words. By God's grace it seldom fails. I think this is a good place to start because it provides the highest return for the least investment—an important element of any introduction. Remember: it is much easier to get people who have experienced the Bible's relevance to study it than it is to get people who study the Bible to experience its relevance. The African Bible study method has several variations, but all of them assume that the text has something to say and that listening people can hear it speak to their lives. Those who have heard it speak know that if they learn more about it they will be better able to hear what it has to say. What is more, this method is practiced in a welcoming environment that builds community without the kind of discussion that often makes newcomers feel diminished. Teaching people to listen to scripture, as the African Bible study method does, is a good place to begin.

When we begin to want to learn more about the Bible, the church of the twenty-first century has multiple blessings. We have a wealth of writings from the scholars of previous generations, with numerous commentaries and study Bibles available to us, and we have a unique opportunity to hear from those traditions that are beginning to enrich our church in new ways. African, African American, indigenous, Asian, and Hispanic voices are being heard with a clarity unsurpassed in previous years. The Episcopal Church's search for meaning in the twenty-first century has the benefit of multiple readings coming from the perspectives of our brothers and sisters in the faith. Immigrant communities and those with recent experiences of marginalization and persecution read the Bible in a different way from those who have borne the mantle and responsibilities of establishment. The Exodus story, the crucifixion, the huddled fears of the persecuted church, and the bold decision of the Jerusalem church to include Gentiles: all these passages are read differently by those with different histories, and each reading has a story to tell the whole church. That is why intellectual modesty is a must. No one perspective or the experience of any one group has a corner on God's Word, and there is no one in our church or any church who cannot learn from the experiences of others. We all struggle to know the universal truths in the circumstances of our own history. We all have a lot of listening to do.

A Guide for
Discussion

You may of course read the books in this series on your own, but because they focus on the transformation of the Episcopal Church in the twenty-first century the books are especially useful as a basis for discussion and reflection within a congregation or community. The questions below are intended to generate fruitful discussion about an experience of the Bible in the congregations with which members of the group are familiar.

Each group will identify its own needs and will be shaped by the interests of the participants and their comfort in sharing personal life stories. Discussion leaders will wish to focus on particular areas that address the concerns and goals of the group, using the questions and themes provided here simply as suggestions for a place to start the conversation.

The Bible as Meeting Ground

In this chapter Wade uses the analogy of the Bible and a book about swimming: "Such a book could tell us much about the physics of water displacement, the manner in which various aquatic creatures move about, the disciplines of Olympic athletes, and the joys of pool and pond. But the study of swimming can take us just so far. At some point the book must be put down and the water entered. Our own faith seeks such a moment" (pp. 15–16).

+ What aspects of Bible study are similar to the process of learning the physics and dynamics of swimming? Why are they important to learn? Where and how did you learn them?

+ When have you "put down" your Bible and "entered the water"? How was your life changed or your faith deepened by the experience?

+ + + + +

Wade notes that the books of the Bible were chosen in the midst of conflict and serious cultural and political problems, to "help form identity in tumultuous and confusing times" (p. 30). He therefore has confidence that the "ancient truths of scripture" will "guide us through the uncharted waters of the twenty-first century" (p. 31).

+ In what ways do you see the Bible's "ancient truths" guiding the church today?

+ How does the church recognize and receive the guidance of scripture?

+ What are some of the barriers to our hearing and acting on the truths of the Bible today?

The Art of Effective Bible Study

In this chapter Wade describes Anglican's "three-legged stool" of scripture, tradition, and reason, and notes that the "conversation" among them "works best when the deeper rhythms and wider truths of the Bible are allowed to speak to the experiences of life" (p. 47).

◆ What are some of the "deeper rhythms" and "wider truths" of the Bible? How do you identify them?

◆ How does tradition and reason inform or challenge your interpretation of "difficult" passages in the Bible, such as the acceptance of slavery (Ephesians 6:5–8); the mandate for genocide (Deuteronomy 20:10–18); or the silencing of women in worship (1 Timothy 2:11–15)?

◆　◆　◆　◆　◆

Wade affirms the importance of the community of faith as "the repository of scripture, tradition, and reason, the interpreter of experience, the setting for the sacraments, and the home of our companions in the meeting ground where God is known" (p. 50).

◆ Describe an occasion in which the community of faith has changed your understanding of a passage or basic truth of the Bible.

◆ When have you been affected or harmed by the "bad fruit" that developed from a biblical interpretation that you believe is misguided or wrong?

◆ If our "theophanies" and interpretations of scripture need the validation of a community (see p. 56), how does that happen, practically speaking? How do we "hear" our community?

Surveying the Methods

In this chapter Wade distinguishes between "methods" and "systems" in studying the Bible: methods are about "*moving* along a path," while systems are about "*taking a stand.*" He notes that "in a method we know the path but not the answer we will find. In a system we know the answer and are showing the path by which one might come to it" (p. 59).

♦ Describe a time in which you encountered a system of Bible study. What was the "stand" that was taken? How was the Bible used to support that stand?

♦ Describe a time in which you encountered a method of Bible study. What "path" was followed? Where did it lead?

♦ ♦ ♦ ♦ ♦

Revisit the principles of Anglican Bible study that Wade outlines on page 61.

♦ Do these principles reflect the experiences you have had of reading the Bible in your congregation? in your personal study?

♦ If you have studied the Bible in non-religious settings or in other Christian traditions, how did their approach to scripture differ from the principles outlined here? What did you find most helpful in those different approaches? What was lacking?

♦ Do you have experience with any of the methods described in this chapter? In what ways did they express the Anglican principles Wade outlines? What other methods have you found to be effective? Why?

Rethinking Our Attitudes

In this chapter Wade considers our underlying assumptions regarding God and the Bible. He describes these attitudes as "embedded theology": they are "our unexamined ideas about life, faith, and God," and are "distinct from 'deliberative theology'—the ideas we have really worked on and figured out in a systematic way" (p. 105).

+ How would you describe the basic principles of your "embedded theology"?

+ What preconceived ideas about God or the Bible have you discovered when you have encountered suffering, your own or others'?

+ What preconceived ideas about God or the Bible have you discovered when you have encountered success or abundance, your own or others'?

◆　◆　◆　◆　◆

Wade quotes C. S. Lewis as noting that "two heads are better than one, not because they are infallible but because they are unlikely to go wrong in the same direction" (p. 107).

+ When has the church's tradition or the witness of other faith traditions caused you to rethink your understanding of God or the Bible?

+ When have scientific discoveries caused you to rethink your understanding of God or the Bible?

+ When have changes in your experience of culture or society caused you to rethink your understanding of God or the Bible?

Stories from the Meeting Ground

In this chapter Wade tells the stories of churches that have creatively engaged the Bible and been transformed by it through listening to the stories of others.

 * When have you experienced the power of the Bible to bring reconcilation in the midst of conflict? Describe how the Bible was used to resolve the disagreements.

 * When have you experienced the power of the Bible to divide a community? Describe how the Bible was used to create or exacerbate the divisions.

 * What are some of the differences between these two experiences of conflict? How can the Bible both unite and divide us?

◆　◆　◆　◆　◆

Wade concludes this chapter with a question: "Episcopalians have all of the pieces in place for a powerful experience with the Bible—so why are we not characterized by such experiences?" (p. 135).

 * How would you answer his question?

 * Have you ever told someone about an experience of God you had or an insight you received while reading the Bible? What was the response? If not, why have you chosen not to speak of that experience?

 * What would it take for you to develop a discipline of Bible study that is characterized by "regular, expectant reading of the Word" (p. 136)? What is stopping you?

Resources

THE ALPHA COURSE
www.alphana.org
Alpha USA / 2275 Half Day Road, Suite 185
Bannockburn, IL 60015 / 888-949-2574

BIBLE WORKBENCH
www.educationalcenter.org
The Educational Center / 6357 Clayton Road
St. Louis, MO 63177 / 800-624-4644

CATECHESIS OF THE GOOD SHEPHERD
www.cgsusa.org
P. O. Box 1084 / Oak Park, IL 60304
708-524-1210

DISCIPLES OF CHRIST IN COMMUNITY (DOCC)
www.cathedral.org/cathedral/programs/docc.shtml
Washington National Cathedral
Mount St. Alban / Washington, DC 20016

EDUCATION FOR MINISTRY
www.sewanee.edu/EFM/
The University of the South / 335 Tennessee Avenue
Sewanee, TN 37383-0001 / 800-722-1974

GODLY PLAY
www.godlyplay.org
The Center for the Theology of Childhood
535 West Roses Road / San Gabriel, CA 91775
626-282-3066

Godly Play Resources
P.O. Box 563 / Ashland, KS 67831 / 800-445-4390

Godly Play Curriculum
www.livingthegoodnews.com
Church Publishing Incorporated
445 Fifth Avenue / New York, New York 10016
800-824-1813

GOSPEL BASED DISCIPLESHIP
www.episcopalchurch.org/ethnic.htm
Native American Ministries, Episcopal Church Center
815 Second Avenue / New York, New York 10017
800-334-7626

IGNATIAN SPIRITUALITY
www.bc.edu/centers/cis/
The Center for Ignatian Spirituality at Boston College
Rahner House / 96 College Road
Chestnut Hill, MA 02467 / 617-552-1777

LESSON PLANS FOR SMALL CONGREGATIONS
www.episcopalchurch.org/
50534_50646_ENG_HTM.htm
Ministries with Young People, Episcopal Church Center
815 Second Avenue / New York, New York 10017
800-334-7626

---

books on the Bible

Anne Barton, *The Daily Office: Exploring Patterns for Daily Prayer and Bible Study* (Cambridge: Grove Books, 1999).

Bart D. Ehrman, *Misquoting Jesus: The Story Behind Who Changed the Bible and Why* (San Francisco: Harper SanFrancisco, 2005).

Roger Ferlo, *Opening the Bible,* Volume 2 in the New Church's Teaching Series (Cambridge, Mass.: Cowley Publications, 1997).

Peter J. Gomes, *The Scandalous Gospel of Jesus: What's So Good About the Good News?* (New York: HarperOne, 2007).

Michael Johnston, *Engaging the Word,* Volume 3 in the New Church's Teaching Series (Cambridge, Mass.: Cowley Publications, 1998).

Donald Kraus, *Sex, Sacrifice, Shame, and Smiting: Is the Bible Always Right?* (New York: Church Publishing, 2008).

Donn Morgan, *Fighting with the Bible: Why Scripture Divides Us and How It Can Bring Us Together* (New York: Church Publishing, 2007).

Jaroslav Pelikan, *Whose Bible Is It? A History of the Scriptures Through the Ages* (New York: Viking, 2005).

Macrina Scott, *Picking the Right Bible Study Program* (Chicago, ACTA Publications, 1992).

Martin Smith, *The Word is Very Near You: A Guide to Praying with Scripture* (Cambridge, Mass.: Cowley Publications, 1989).

Norvene Vest, *No Moment Too Small: Rhythms of Silence, Prayer, and Holy Reading* (Cambridge, Mass.: Cowley Publications, 1994). (See especially the chapter on *lectio divina*.)

Walter Wink, *The Bible in Human Transformation: Toward a New Paradigm for Bible Study* (Philadelphia: Fortress Press, 1973). (A study guide was published in 1980.)

N.T. Wright, *The Last Word: Beyond the Bible Wars to a New Understanding of the Authority of Scripture* (San Francisco: HarperSanFrancisco, 2005).

Notes and Sources

notes

1. Quoted in "Baptismal covenant forms foundation for Title III revisions" by Mary Frances Schjonberg, Episcopal News Service, July 2004 (www.episcopalchurch.org/3577_17290_ENG_HTM.htm).
2. Marion Hatchett, *Commentary on the American Prayer Book* (New York: Seabury Press, 1980), 251.
3. Nathan Hatch, *The Democratization of American Christianity* (New Haven, Conn.: Yale University Press, 1989), 112.
4. The complete text for Sojourner Truth's speech "Ain't I a Woman" can be found in the Internet Modern History Sourcebook: www.fordham.edu/halsall/mod/sojtruth-woman.html.
5. Rowan Williams, "The Bible: Reading and Hearing," Larkin-Stuart Lecture co-sponsored by Trinity College and St. Thomas Anglican Church, Toronto, Canada, April 16, 2007; see the complete text at www.trinity.utoronto.ca/News_Events/News/archbishop.htm.
6. William Porcher DuBose, *High Priesthood and Sacrifice* (1908), quoted in *They Still Speak: Readings for the Lesser Feasts,* ed. J. Robert Wright (New York: Church Publishing, 1993), 153.
7. Williams, "The Bible."
8. Margot Critchfield, personal correspondence with the author, February 28, 2008.
9. Dorothy Linthicum, *Episcopal Teacher,* Center for the Ministry of Teaching, Virginia Theological Seminary (Fall 2007).

10. Patricia Coulter, Gianna Gobbi, and Silvana Montanzro, *The Good Shepherd and the Child: A Joyful Journey*, ed. Sofia Cavalletti (Chicago: Archdiocese of Chicago Liturgy Training Publications, 2003), 90.

11. Mark Twain, *Letters from the Earth III* (New York: Harper and Row, 1974), 20.

12. Frederick Buechner, *Wishful Thinking* (San Francisco: HarperSanFrancisco, 1973, 1993), 9.

13. C. S. Lewis, "On the Reading of Old Books," in *God in the Dock*, ed. Walter Hooper (Grand Rapids: Eerdmans, 1970), 201–202.

14. Fred Vergara, *Mainstreaming: Asian Americans in the Episcopal Church* (New York: Office of Asian Ministries, Episcopal Church Center, 2005), 133–136.

15. Mark McDonald, from his *Introduction to Rites of Passage*, in the Report of the Standing Commission on Liturgy and Music to the 75th General Convention, page 142.

16. McDonald, *Introduction*, 141.

17. Quoted in *Renewing the Stuff of Life* by Cynthia B. Cohen (New York: Oxford University Press, 2007), 95.

---

sources

Quotations set apart within the chapters have been taken from the following books and articles.

Verna Dozier, *Equipping the Saints* (Washington, D.C.: The Alban Institute, 1981).

William Porcher DuBose, *High Priesthood and Sacrifice* (New York, 1908); quoted in *They Still Speak: Readings for the Lesser Feasts*, ed. J. Robert Wright (New York: Church Hymnal, 1993), 153.

Richard Hooker, *Laws of Ecclesiastical Polity*, III.8.10.

Norvene Vest, *No Moment Too Small: Rhythms of Silence, Prayer, and Holy Reading* (Cambridge, Mass.: Cowley Publications, 1994), 78.

Rowan Williams, "The Bible: Reading and Hearing," Larkin-Stuart Lecture, April 16, 2007; www.trinity.utoronto.ca/ News_Events/News/archbishop.htm.